MW00329312

TALES OF THE HONEY BADGER

NICK CUMMINS

With a Foreword by
Emeritus Professor Roland Sussex OAM

ABC
Books

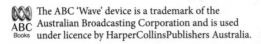 The ABC 'Wave' device is a trademark of the Australian Broadcasting Corporation and is used under licence by HarperCollinsPublishers Australia.

First published in Australia in 2015
by HarperCollinsPublishers Australia Pty Limited
ABN 36 009 913 517
harpercollins.com.au

Copyright © Nick Cummins 2015

The right of Nick Cummins to be identified as the author of this work has been asserted by him in accordance with the *Copyright Amendment (Moral Rights) Act 2000*.

This work is copyright. Apart from any use as permitted under the Copyright Act 1968, no part may be reproduced, copied, scanned, stored in a retrieval system, recorded, or transmitted, in any form or by any means, without the prior written permission of the publisher.

HarperCollins*Publishers*
Level 13, 201 Elizabeth Street, Sydney, NSW 2000, Australia
Unit D1, 63 Apollo Drive, Rosedale, Auckland 0632, New Zealand
A 53, Sector 57, Noida, UP, India
1 London Bridge Street, London, SE1 9GF, United Kingdom
2 Bloor Street East, 20th floor, Toronto, Ontario M4W 1A8, Canada
195 Broadway, New York, NY 10007

National Library of Australia Cataloguing-in-Publication data:

Cummins, Nick, 1987– author.
  Tales of the Honey Badger / Nick Cummins.
  ISBN: 9780733334726 (paperback)
  Subjects: Cummins, Nick, 1987 – Anecdotes.
  Cummins, Nick, 1987 – Humor.
  Rugby Union football players – Australia – Humor.
  Australian wit and humor.
796.333092

Cover and internal design by Hazel Lam, HarperCollins Design Studio
Front cover images: Nick Cummins by Daniel Wilkins/Newspix; all other images by shutterstock.com
Back cover images courtesy of the author
Typeset in Minion Pro by Kirby Jones
Printed and bound in Australia by Griffin Press
The papers used by HarperCollins in the manufacture of this book are natural, recyclable product made from wood grown in sustainable plantation forests. The fibre source and manufacturing processes meet recognised international environmental standards, and carry certification.

BEFORE WE GET STARTED

In order for the ship to reach its next port, it has to consider the weather. Wind (like people) comes from all directions. It hits you head-on to slow or teach you and from the back to encourage you to realise your potential. Waves come in the form of family illness, non-selection and self-doubt that test your resilience. But there are also waves of success – reward for your hard work, and one must ride these with humility and awareness of who you are and where you came from.

Social media and journalism are like a submerged reef, waiting for you to make a mistake. The public (even those who support you) can't help themselves but to splash your actions over the web.

After nine years playing professional rugby, I can say the real gift that came to me in the form of refreshing rain is that of giving! Firstly giving back to those who put the wind in my sails. Then giving people the energy they gave me, red skies and cloudless starry nights. The whole Badger business would be nothing without these people.

This story began with inspiration drawn from my old man's video tapes showing him running around mad as a cut snake with his head taped up. I think because he never spoke about it, I was all the more intrigued about his former life.

I played under 7's for the Sunnybank Dragons. The only game I can remember was having a penalty try awarded against me for tackling in a two-hand touch game (worth it). The next time I played was in high school under my two coaches Mr Rhodes and Mr Bricknell (both good fellas). Our school comp was short and fairly average and being the only *palangi* (white boy) in my team, I had to step up. They were big kids, some with beards at 13. That could be why we smashed every other team in the comp by 60. By year 12 I had finally grown enough to assert occasional dominance at training.

For two years I would fly up to Bundaberg to play important games for the Buccaneers alongside my brother Luke. In 2005 my two older brothers and I won the Grand Final and after the game, Mr Wise (a Randwick scout) approached my bro Luke. Between them it was organised to launch me to Sydney for a trial. A big thank you to both Luke and Mr Wise for sorting what would be the beginning of a tough road.

Arriving in Sydney I was greeted by Keith Homes who put me on to the accommodation and a contact for work. Thanks Keith for the work you did for the players and club, a lot of it went unnoticed and unrewarded.

I began work in a factory for a bloke who was a hair-raising bit of gear, Carl McDonald. Amongst the players this man was feared as any backchat would result in his already red face going crimson and his hair would somehow turn whiter followed by 400m sprints for all. This man gave me a job and put me on a demanding additional training schedule. Tough man in the game, but outside of that, a generous good bloke who would go into bat for ya.

After my training I was ready to take on the trials for the Australian Sevens coached by Glen Ella. Glen took a chance and picked me as the only Colts player for the Dubai and South Africa tour where it turns out he's a good bloke that you can have a beer or seven with, thanks mate.

I signed my first rookie contract with Western Force coaches John Mitchell and John Mulvihill. Thanks to Mitch for my first crack at Super Rugby and Mulvers for being a coach that was one of the boys as well.

Robbie Deans selected me for my first Wallaby squad and for my debut versus the Pumas. It took a couple of years of convincing him but not a bad Kiwi in my book. He recently coached the World 15 which I was gratefully part of, thanks mate.

Thanks Snoz for the Commonwealth Games, didn't learn much except how to get loose, it was great. Ewen McKenzie, aside from how the Ireland incident with the 'Dublin Six' was handled, he's not a bad bloke – you never know what someone's going through so be kind to all. Michael Cheika, you understand the importance of the mind and incorporate that in training well. Thanks for teaching me those things. If you pick me for the RWC I owe ya a beer, if not we can still have a beer but we won't talk about it. Thanks to Shogo Mukai San of Coca Cola Red Sparks for making it possible to play two seasons a year. The current coach of Cola has been great and has enabled me to continue with my commercial opportunities, thank you Tomo San.

My Commercial Partnerships Manager, Josh White, has worked tirelessly behind the scenes to align me with the right opportunities and helped shaped the path for the days after rugby. He's like family to me, and even though he likes to ride me like Seabiscuit at times, I appreciate the effort, thanks mate.

I met a bloke, Blair Frendin ten years ago in Colts and I'm still good mates with him today. He dealt with my shit behaviour during the stressful tough times of rugby and always offered his time and energy when needed. We've been on a few tours over the years but the best is yet to come, thanks Blair balls.

Girlfriends, they turn up unannounced and teach you a few lessons about girls and about yourself. Recently I did a little reflecting on past relationships and I realised I'd been an ungrateful muppet at times. Thanks girls for putting up with me during those youthful stages. It turns out, don't try change a girl, she's beautiful in her own way.

All my family has had something to do with any success I've had, but just to name a couple (not enough pages in the this book) Liz and Joe, I'm sorry if this brings unwanted attention but I just want to say this whole media rubbish doesn't mean anything compared to how much I respect you two. It's humbling and empowering how you face adversity, I love you so much and thank you for (unknowingly) teaching me about life and its obstacles, you two have given me strength in times I had none.

Mum, although your religious beliefs are pretty strong, you have shown wisdom and faith on what's important. You have put up with a lot – having eight kids is a big effort. I've missed you Mum, know that I love you and you will always be in my prayers.

Dad, you've had a lot to deal with and have held the side together well. We are all grateful and I really appreciate your help with this book. You're a weird unit and part-time mad bastard and I hold you dearly.

A massively important part of this book's completion comes down to the great work of Josh Rakic. I've got the grammar and spelling skills of a 9 yr old, so Josh R was put under enormous pressure – hey, they say that's where diamonds are formed. I don't care what they say about ya, I think you're alright. Your pressie is in the mail.

And finally to ABC Books and HarperCollins, should be a good book, but I'll thank you when it's out, to avoid the embarrassment.

Can't hear a fat lady, I've got some gear planned for the future, stay tuned.

The Badger

CONTENTS

"HOLY TOMORRA. HOW GOOD? BLOODY, YOU BEAUTY.

"

Translation: 'I'm too excited to speak coherently.'

FOREWORD – THE BADGER'S TONGUE

Nick Cummins is a one-off. He's a fast fluent footballer. He's a fast fluent footballer with a fast fluent tongue. He's a fast fluent footballer with a fast fluent Australian tongue. It's the combination of those properties which makes him unique.

If you interview a footballer at the end of a game, most of them are too exhausted to go much beyond reliable clichés: 'We knew it was going to be a tough one, they took it down to the wire, the boys dug deep, we're glad to have the 3 points'. Or the 4 points, or whatever. To be sure, to be sure. Let them head off to the showers.

Nick Cummins is quite otherwise. Not for him the stolid cliché. He's a larrikin both in sport and in English, a spontaneous sports bard. His language has moments of startling poetry. It crackles with the unexpected, or with nuggets of Australian colloquial English. Like the origin of his nickname. He saw a video of a honey badger – a notably feisty small animal – attack a lion:

'He tore the canastas off the big fella'

and the lion retreated, bled out and died. It's the implacable determination in the face of odds that gave Nick Cummins his

Honey Badger name, and some of the character of what he does on the football field.

The Badger is a terrific example of the sense of play and fun for which Australian English has become famous. He interviews with a characteristic grin and obvious enjoyment. He's a showman, on and off the field, on and off the tongue.

His style of talking has three main features.

The first part of his repertoire is **rhyming slang**. Australians got this from the Cockneys in the East End of London, and it's taken unshakeable root Down Under:

'I just saw the line, pinned me ears back and ended bagging a bit of meat in the corner there, which was tops!'

'Meat'? Meat pie – try. Like 'Give us a Captain Cook' for 'give us a look'. That's the ordinary kind of rhyming slang. Then you take away the rhyming word, so 'Give us a Captain' is all you get, and you have to find a likely captain, aka Captain Cook, and then rebuild what the person is saying, or not saying, from the rhyme. That's what HB does: he doesn't say 'meat pie', but he deletes the rhyming word and we have to do the work to recover the rest.

The second feature of the Honey Badger's talking success is the **simile** – comparisons using the words 'like' or 'as'. This is another famous feature of Australian English. We have hundreds of them: 'mad as a cut snake', 'strong as a Mallee bull', 'as useless as ...' with many useless things to follow, some not in the best taste.

As with rhyming slang, the Badger pushes similes to the limit. 'Off like a bride's nightie' means that someone has gone or left in a hurry. But that's not enough for HB. He teams it up with another common Australian expression:

'Last year we were all sizzle and no steak, but now we're off like a bride's nightie.'

Political correctness? Ignore it:

'As straight as a Mardi Gras.'

Social comment?:

'As full as Centrelink on payday.'

RSPCA?

'Sweating like a bag of cats at a greyhound meet.'

And the third property of his talk is cheerful, wilful, perverse, good humoured ***leg-pulling and irreverence***:

'You uh ever heard of that bible story of Samson and Delilah? – Well, it's got nothing to do with what I'm doing, so...'

The Honey Badger's speech is deliberate, whimsical, teasing, good-humoured, quizzical and prolific. He's playing to the audience in language the way he plays to the audience on the field. He knows he's being provocative, and invites us to join the joke.

And what is the motive behind all this fun with language? As he put it:

'It's a bit of genuinity, if that's a word.'

And why not?

Roland Sussex OAM
Emeritus Professor of Applied Language Studies
University of Queensland

FORCE V TAHS POST-MATCH:

" YOU GOTTA BE LIKE A MIDGET IN A URINAL – YOU GOTTA BE ON YOUR TOES. "

TRANSLATION: 'With many establishments having forgone the classic trough in favour of the individual wall-mounted urinal, people who stand shorter than average are left with no choice but to stand on their toes to relieve themselves without making a mess of the bathroom or themselves.'

THE FIRST CUMMINS

1987, Australia. It was a year of many firsts in this great land of ours. Austen Tayshus' mate Boomer rang from a mobile phone for the first time, Kylie Minogue – whose advances I've reluctantly refused on several occasions – shot to the top of the charts with 'I Should Be So Lucky' and we co-hosted the very first Rugby World Cup.

Of course, the star-studded Wallabies lost to France that year and coach Alan Jones put the desperate plea out to the entire nation to offer up their first-born sons for the good of the cause.

And that was good enough for my old man, Mark. Within a matter of months, I broke the line for the very first time on October 5, 1987. Okay, so the maths doesn't quite work out. But as you'll find out in the 200-odd pages to come, I rarely let the

I WAS A BIG UNIT. HIT THE EARTH AT AROUND 10 POUNDS AND WASN'T SHORT OF ADMIRERS IF I REMEMBER CORRECTLY.

truth get in the way of a good yarn. If this book were a movie, it'd be prefixed with 'based on true events'. And named something powerful like *Unit: Rip and Tear.*

Admittedly, that's probably not the greatest segue back to the day of my birth on that glorious October morning in Port Macquarie. But it paints a picture, nonetheless.

I was a big unit. Hit the earth at around 10 pounds and wasn't short of admirers if I remember correctly. Some say babies can't remember that far back but I never forget a good break.

And from what I'm told I was hard on the tooth from day one, loved the tucker and loved life. I was No. 4 of eight kids – just missed out on the medal.

Mum gave Dad a full backline but demanded a stop to it at No. 8. And I don't think he's ever quite forgiven her for not going the extra mile and producing the forwards to complete the roster. But with Bernadette, Luke and Nathan in front of me and Leish, Lizzy, Jake and Joe behind me, we weren't short of a scrum.

Life was pretty simple. Dad was a schoolteacher and Mum occasionally did some part-time teaching, too – the woman hates sleeping is the only thing I can surmise – so we had plenty of holidays to the beach and no shortage of company.

The old man played rugby for Port, so I was introduced to the game at an early age. But what I remember most is that he'd pull a hamstring to get off the field and home in time for *Hey Hey It's Saturday!* With our starting 10 plus whichever friends and relatives were playing off the bench, our lounge room had more chairs than Officeworks. And when *Hey Hey!* was on, there wasn't a spare seat in the house. Personally, I didn't have a Scooby Doo what everyone was laughing at but I just took the lead from which ever kid was next to me.

Tweed Heads soon became home before the old man finally got sick of staring at rooms full of kids. We made the shift up north to Brisbane where he got into the pool business. Shameless plug: When you want to turn your backyard into paradise, call Amazon Landscapes on 0418 192 619.

Better yet, prank call the bloke. He loves that.

Anyhow, suffice to say, we weren't short of a pool growing up and some bloody big ones at that. I remember one in particular, with a giant cave and waterfall to boot. There was something about being in a cave that just felt right – primal. It resonated with me. And, of course, it was a perfect hiding place from which

I DIDN'T MIND SCHOOL BUT I WAS NEVER GOING TO BE A ROCKET SCIENTIST. HELL, THE WORLD HAD HEAPS OF THOSE ALREADY.

to scare the living Brad Pitt out of any poor bugger that thought they'd take some time out to enjoy the serenity. What a buzz!

I was slowly becoming one of the big kids. And I was loving my rugby. In fact, more so because it was an excuse to get out of the classroom.

I didn't mind school but I was never going to be a rocket scientist. Hell, the world had heaps of those already.

Even back then I looked at things a bit differently to everyone else. I could always be relied upon – and still am – to ask the questions that no one seemed to be able to answer – like, if a tree falls in the woods, does a bear hear it?

So rugby was never the be-all and end-all for me. It was simply an escape. I played a few games at school and got a start in the Queensland Schoolboys II team. With a big islander population, I was the token white unit in the side. And alongside those big lads – who had more muscle tone at 16 than I've managed to attain even now – I looked premature by comparison.

Our coach, Mr Hopenoa, was a good bloke and taught me a lot. But by the time school finished I was no stand-out. I never envisaged turning rugby into a career.

BY THE TIME SCHOOL FINISHED I WAS NO STAND-OUT. I NEVER ENVISAGED TURNING RUGBY INTO A CAREER

I worked for the old boy doing landscaping but just as Cain killed Abel, the hard work was killing me. I didn't know what I wanted to do with my life. I was like an immigrant Nigerian in the heart of Sydney – lost, and hoping for millions in inheritance from my long-lost royal relatives.

THE TURNING POINT

That money from the Nigerian royal family still hadn't come through. So, as I waited for the cheque to clear, I headed up north to Bundaberg to visit my eldest brother, Luke, who was captain of the East Coast Buccaneers.

At least, that's what I told him. My sole intention was to make a beeline for the Bundy Rum distillery, but in an effort to afford the goods, I offered to play a few games for the Buccaneers to help out.

It was country rugby at its best – boat races, peculiar dressing room behaviour and many strange events (which you might hear about later). God, it was good. I was in my element. And I must have gone all right because no sooner had I pulled on my best singlet and thongs to head to the distillery than a bloke tapped me on the shoulder and asked me to come with him to Sydney.

Now, even for the Bundy dressing rooms, this was an unusual proposition. But when he explained he had links to Randwick Rugby Club, I thought to myself, 'Why the bloody hell not? Dad can go Michael Luck his shovel. I'm in!'

I got a start in the Colts team and it wasn't long before half the first-grade side pissed off to the Waratahs for the Super Rugby season and I got my first crack at first-grade Sydney rugby. And I loved it.

NOW, EVEN FOR THE BUNDY DRESSING ROOMS, THIS WAS AN UNUSUAL PROPOSITION.

SEVENS SELECTION

Well, my enthusiasm must have shown. And all that manual labour with the old man had me in half-decent shape – even if I do say so myself. And with Rugby Sevens on the cusp of becoming an Olympic sport, the Sevens game was on the up – and Glen Ella needed players.

I would have simply been happy with his autograph (which he gave to me begrudgingly to shut me up) but to have a Wallabies legend like him pick me to represent my country, I was like a fireplace on a romantic winter's night – stoked!

A matter of months after a chance encounter in Bundy, I was on a plane with the Australian Sevens

I WAS LIKE A FIREPLACE ON A ROMANTIC WINTER'S NIGHT – STOKED!

and some Wallabies legends headed for Wellington, New Zealand. It was shock and awe stuff. I was in awe of everyone around me and the opportunity that I'd been presented with. And in shock because New Zealand wasn't considered an international flight and therefore booze was an out-of-pocket expense. Not that any rugby team ever drinks during transit… In fact, I wanna take this opportunity to give a quick shout-out to Bill Pulver and Michael Cheika – Billy, Check, if you're reading this, I've never consumed a single drop of alcohol while on tour. Swear. But if you give me a buzz, I can tell you three wingers in the current Wallabies squad who have.

Jokes aside, my old man was in no laughing mood when I told him the good news. Largely because I didn't call him until the plane had already taken off. And even then, it was only to get his credit card details so I could afford a drink – of juice. Like when I lost my virginity, my memories of the game are hazy at best. I was so caught up in the whole experience that everything just flew by. But I'm told I was outstanding. Went all right on the field, too…

SOMETHING STINKS

What I remember most vividly from that trip is the whole tour experience and the good times I had rooming with Blair Connor. One of us had some serious wind issues and let's just say, the hotel maid didn't take it too kindly. We were two little shit teenagers from Brisbane with no parental supervision and poo and fart jokes were our bread and butter – as they should be for any teenager. Or adult…

If we weren't chicken leg fighting or attempting to lure each other into invisible clouds of our personal scents, we were trying to prank each other. And unfortunately, there were civilian casualties – that poor maid.

She'd arrived one morning eager to clean our room – or burn it – and get the hell out of there. Come to think of it, there was enough natural gas in that place that a naked flame could well have spelled the end for all of us.

Well, having just enjoyed his morning bowl of fibre, Blair had taken up seat at the throne to stick to true to his painfully strict ritual. So of course, I requested the maid 'start with the bathroom first'. And in she went – poor bastard.

I REQUESTED THE MAID 'START WITH THE BATHROOM FIRST'. AND IN SHE WENT – POOR BASTARD.

The screams were simultaneous. Blair was plain shocked. Whereas the maid was shocked by the smell. In fact, given she immediately began dry-retching, it's safe to say she was disgusted. I can't be sure but I swear only one word came out of her mouth before her breakfast quickly followed – 'Ungodly'. I've been on the do-not-room-with list ever since.

UNITED ARAB MANKINI

If New Zealand was good, then Dubai was great. I'm a big fan of terry towelling and that stuff was everywhere. But seriously, to experience such a vastly different culture from what I'd grown up with was something I'll always remember. And what I'll never forget is that heat – and what it inspired me to do.

The UAE is pretty strict on dress codes for men and women. But especially the fairer sex. And I'll be damned if a woman doesn't have a right to wear a bikini wherever the hell she wants to.

You'll never hear me mutter the words 'cover up'. unless my makeup artist asks my preferred brand of eye liner.

> **I'LL BE DAMNED IF A WOMAN DOESN'T HAVE A RIGHT TO WEAR A BIKINI WHEREVER THE HELL SHE WANTS TO.**

Anyhow, Dubai ain't got no laws on men wearing bikinis at the beach. So with Sacha Baron-Cohen's *Borat* still fresh in my mind – as is the fury at The Academy for robbing him of the Best Actor award – I took a stand. Like Clark Kent to Superman, I disappeared to a dark dark corner – a cocoon, if you will – dropped the team suit and re-emerged a beautiful butterfly. Complete with fluoro mankini.

My luscious mane was at ultimate volume. My body devoid of all hair. And it must have been the bright green combined with the heat, but even the baby badger looked respectable. Suffice to say, confidence was at an all-time high.

As such, I took to the sand like a teenage girl to Instagram and performed a flamboyant, erotic sprint and swan dive into the water.

It felt a little weird having the eyes of the world on me but what the hell? They do it in Sydney at the Mardi Gras and no one gives a rats. If anything, I'm more disappointed no one's extended an offer to join a float.

A FORCE TO BE RECKONED WITH PART: 1

With the Sevens box ticked and giving it my all at Randwick, the possibility of turning this rugby thing into a career was starting to creep onto my radar. I never had the hype of a young hotshot nor was I some widely-acclaimed prodigy. I was a toiler and I bloody enjoyed the team atmosphere and doing whatever I could, whenever I could, to get us across the line.

THE POSSIBILITY OF TURNING THIS RUGBY THING INTO A CAREER WAS STARTING TO CREEP ONTO MY RADAR.

I never expected 'the call' but sure enough, one fateful Matraville day, after the third of seven police cars had visited my building for one reason or the other, the phone rang. My first thought? 'F*&k me. Who paid the phone bill?' My second thought: 'For the love of God, please don't be Telstra'.

I'd received offers from both the NSW Waratahs and Western Force. They wanted to give me a go. 'Look out. The Badge is about to go prime time.'

I was ecstatic. Happier than a mosquito in a blood bank. The Force told me to hit the frog and toad and bring the old man along to see what the West was all about.

I WAS ECSTATIC. HAPPIER THAN A MOSQUITO IN A BLOOD BANK.

And compared to Sydney, Perth was lawless. There was open space, hipsters were at a minimum and the entire city and surrounding suburbs were easier to navigate than a single block in Sydney. Let's be honest, Sydney roads are like a maze on the back of a Happy Meal completed by a three-year-old. It's a mess.

So there was a lot to like and when it came down to negotiations, the old man had just what it took to make a deal – absolutely no idea and blind confidence. It's the winner's way; a method that's made generations of Australians millions. Matter of fact, there could be a TED Talk in that…

Anyhow, later that arvo – and with NSW still an option – the old man grabbed a six-pack of Crownies and we sat together on the deck to watch the sun set over the water. The romanticism was lost on me, but by the time the old boy knocked off five of the beers he was in love. The deal was done. I was staying in Perth and making my Super Rugby debut for the Western Force.

ORIGIN OF THE HONEY BADGER

Not a day goes past where some shagger won't ask me where my nickname hails from. And those who haven't witnessed the almighty strength, speed, might, cunning and power of the African Honey Badger typically assume it's because I must look like one. Wrong, lads.

While my golden locks may be 'honey' in colour according to the Revlon colour palette, the honey badger is anything but. It's predominantly black with a white top – think Cadbury Top Deck – and about the size of one of those yappy dogs – only tough.

The little blokes have guts, razor-sharp teeth and claws, and will take

THE LITTLE BLOKES HAVE GUTS, RAZOR-SHARP TEETH AND CLAWS

on anything with the kind of confidence usually reserved for a bloke with a gut-full of tinnies at the town dance.

Bees? Stuff 'em. All the bee stings in the world won't stop a honey badger from getting to the honey pot. Cobra snakes? Please. Honey badgers get bitten by cobra snakes just to prove that aggression is the best medicine. Then kill the bastards and eat 'em just to remind 'em who's boss.

And lions? The supposed 'king of beasts'? Nothing but big pussies when faced with a honey badger.

It was a doco I caught a few years back that first brought my attention to the honey badger. A lion was about to feast on what I considered to be a poor little animal.

For all money, the badge was done for – right before that little bastard turned around, let out a rebel yell and went straight at the big prick's nutsack and ripped his knackers clean off.

The lion hobbled off and kicked the bucket. The badge just trotted off – job done. But there was no Elton John ballad for this fearless bastard. He wouldn't want one. He's not after the limelight.

THERE WAS NO ELTON JOHN BALLAD FOR THIS FEARLESS BASTARD.

It was right there and then I found myself a new favourite animal. A hero. A god if you will. That never-say-die attitude. That aggression. That ability to shake a beating off and get right back up and go again.

And I swore to myself that I would employ all the attributes of the honey badger in my approach to footy – sans the ball-hacking. Don't reckon the refs would take too kindly to that…

As for my chat and quick tongue? Thank the old man for that one. He's been talkin' in riddles as long as I can remember and it just rubbed off.

Guess you could say I'm a colloquial poet but didn't even realise it… Ha. Got ya!

FORCE VS CHIEFS:

"I WAS BUSIER THAN A ONE-ARMED BRICKLAYER IN BAGHDAD. "

TRANSLATION: 'Laying bricks is a hard enough living with two arms, let alone having just one and being expected to do the work of a two-armed man. Baghdad is a particularly ripe terrain for bricklayers, having undergone many aesthetic and structural redesigns in the past three decades.'

THE ROAD TO RAINBOW BEACH

Every school holidays for as long as I can remember, the family made the three-and-a-half-hour journey north to Rainbow Beach – or 'the gateway to Fraser Island' as the more pretentious folk like to call it.

Rainbow's a small coastal town inland of Gympie and north of Noosa that's great for fishing and surfing. It was safe and you could get away with murder there. Which I think is why Mum and Dad took us there. You know, just in case…

And one summer – pun not intended but an exceptional coincidence – he very nearly put me and my sister Bernadette

IT WAS SAFE AND YOU COULD GET AWAY WITH MURDER THERE. WHICH I THINK IS WHY MUM AND DAD TOOK US THERE.

out of our misery when he threatened to turn the car into a tree on account of a Daryl Braithwaite overload.

We loved that Braithwaite tape and Bernadette made sure it played over and over for the near four-hour journey. She actually prayed for traffic so she could hear 'Horses' all over again.

But as if having eight screaming kids in a minivan wasn't enough, there was no way the old man was putting up with some 'sell-out Sherbet drop-out' for the best part of half a day.

He feigned a hard right just to put the scare into us and insisted that if we survived he'd assassinate Daryl Braithwaite. Sorry, Daz.

Speaking of flogging a dead horse, it was the same trip when Mum spotted one by the road. She was already off Dad for threatening to murder-suicide her entire family and it didn't help Dad's cause when he explained to us kids that the reason the horse died was because his parachute mustn't have opened.

That pricked my little ears up. 'Dad, does that happen often?' Mum was more embarrassed than aghast. Looked like her son was going to be a rugby league player…

LOLLY THIEF

Death threats and dead horses aside, I loved that place. The freedom, the smell, the serenity. Just driving into the place gave me a grin like a dead sheep. Hell, I'm starting to detect a theme here… Anyone have a number for a good children's psychiatrist?

Anyway, like any kid, I loved lollies. And back in those days, public hygiene was a matter for the courts – not the local convenience store. You'd grab an empty paper bag, stick your grubby hands into the lolly jars and jam that bag full with all sorts of coloured frogs, race cars, snakes and jubes.

And at the local cafe, the haunt for us 12-year-olds, they worked on the honour system. Fill your

JUST DRIVING INTO THE PLACE GAVE ME A GRIN LIKE A DEAD SHEEP.

bag and tell the cashier how many you had in there. Sounds great in theory, but it's a recipe for disaster when you combine honour, kids and lollies. 'Nick, you genius,' I thought to myself as I crammed that bag full with enough to feed half the Wallabies scrum.

But when the sheila behind the counter scoped my bulging bag and I said all cool-like, '50 cents', she smelt a rat. She then began counting every lolly, one by one, and tallied it up to $7. That's about $300 by today's standards. Needless to say, I was filthy. I told her I was already full anyhow and didn't want them.

Bugger it, my life of crime was over before it ever started. And that was when Diabetes 2 was merely an album title consideration for AC/DC.

CAN'T TELL ME NOTHIN'

With enough kids to fill out an entire basketball roster, keeping an eye on us all was a task new-age parents today couldn't even fathom. No helicopter, single engine plane or hovercraft parenting here. Just some good ol'-fashioned rules. And two loving parents who struck fear inside all of us.

The beach presented the most dangers. We learned about rips, knew how to swim and weren't scared of the water. But even then, Dad had a hard and fast rule – no surfing out the back unless you were old enough and good enough.

Up until I was 12, I was resigned to frolicking around the shore with my little sisters and brother. But come this holiday, I was ready. I couldn't stand being in the shallows and Dad and my older brothers were out the back, carving it up. So I broke protocol.

I didn't care about the consequences – the belt, the jug cord, the ruler or whatever else my parents could conjure up. I needed to be out the back and it was time to prove myself.

So I grabbed a board and paddled straight out, knowing full well Dad wouldn't have a bar of it. Like you react to a salesman at a Chinese market trying to sell you 'good deal' for double the product's value, Dad just laughed, shook his head and pointed to the shore. But I was determined. I screamed out to him, 'I can do this'. And he just grinned. Challenge accepted.

I DIDN'T CARE ABOUT THE CONSEQUENCES – THE BELT, THE JUG CORD, THE RULER OR WHATEVER ELSE MY PARENTS COULD CONJURE UP.

If memory serves correct, I punished the wave like Christian Grey would a sex slave and cemented myself as a 'big kid' there and then.

Looking back, I should never have crossed that threshold. Because what came along with being a big kid was housework, babysitting and having to help Dad with the landscaping. If only I weren't such a talented surfer…

ROCKING UP TO RANDWICK

The old man accompanied me when I relocated to Sydney to play for Randwick. He wanted to see first-hand what I was getting myself into and had heard good things about the pubs.

We were picked up from the airport by Keith Holmes – a great bloke who worked hard for the club and isn't given enough credit – and taken to the accomm to drop my bags.

Walking along Anzac Parade for the first time we were mesmerised. The endless wonder and possibilities of Kingsford… Then we saw coming toward us a large human wearing a short black skirt with tight boob

WALKING ALONG ANZAC PARADE FOR THE FIRST TIME WE WERE MESMERISED.

tube, dangling earrings, a bald head and the biggest Adam's apple I'd ever seen. By Greenbank RSL terms, she was a real looker.

So Dad says with a stupid grin: 'Struth! Look, Nick. Your new neighbour.' Of course, I put him in his place and informed Dad that it's perfectly acceptable that some people are born one specific gender but identify with another. Some say Bruce Jenner got the confidence required to make the transition that very day...

Of course, that was only a taste of the sights and sounds of wonderful Kingsford. We were about to enter the four-level block of old units I'd been assigned to live in when suddenly a large Pacific Islander – Maraki Toa – leaned over the third-level balcony and said: 'Hey, bru. You in here, too?' One look at his surroundings and Dad couldn't help himself: 'When do ya get out?', insinuating the building was a prison. And it was a fair call, because it wasn't far off one.

HE KNEW MY PSYCHE AND WAS USING REVERSE PSYCHOLOGY TO URGE ME TO TAKE THE CHALLENGE AND PROVE HIM WRONG.

After a few beers, a feed and a punt that night – before it was illegal for athletes to do so – Keith dropped me home on his way back to the airport with Dad. It'd been a lot to take in and Dad left me with some very inspiring words: 'Well, good luck, son. I'll see ya in a couple of months when you're back home.' He left me with a chuckle, more or less suggesting I'd give up and head home with my tail between my legs.

But I know now that was classic man management. He knew my psyche and was using reverse psychology to urge me to take the challenge and prove him wrong.

I had saved a small amount of loot from landscape labouring and the new world of money management saw my funds quickly dry up, but crawling back for help was not on!

I was still living out of his old Port Macquarie Pirates rugby bag and during these times, one

DURING THESE TIMES, ONE VEGEMITE SANGA (NO BUTTER) FOR DINNER WASN'T UNCOMMON.

Vegemite sanga (no butter) for dinner wasn't uncommon. But I pushed on. And once my budget was sorted, I was able to eat good tucker again. Souths Juniors did a red-hot T-bone and veggies for $5 and I'd hit three or four of them five or six times a week. The Sunday roast at $7 only became an option a little later. But I firmly believe those meals were a critical factor in making the Australian Sevens squad.

"DUNNO HOW LONG IN ME, BEFORE THE OLD PINS GIVE OUT...THE OLD GETAWAY STICKS."

TRANSLATION: 'I've blown out a few birthday candles in my time and there's really no telling how many good years I have left in my legs before they give out.'

CSI: MATRAVILLE

Adam Ashley-Cooper spends more money on hair and moisturising products than I earned in a full season at Randwick, so suffice to say, times were tough on the old velcro wallet.

I was sharing a very average unit in Matraville with a few mates from the club. The kind of unit they'd find a bloated dead body in on one of those *CSI* shows before deducing from the Home Brand two-minute noodles' point of view that it was murder by way of Playstation altercation. Needless to say, the area was dodgy.

At night, there were fights and screams in 20 different languages – multiculturalism at its best. Like a Weight

AT NIGHT, THERE WERE FIGHTS AND SCREAMS IN 20 DIFFERENT LANGUAGES – MULTICULTURALISM AT ITS BEST.

Watchers client, I could smell all that good tucker – from each of the five continents – and would have torn off my left nut to get a spoonful. But I never got to taste that bloody stuff. The things I would have done to even be in a position to get salmonella…

Alas, I was resigned to surviving on whatever pasta, tinned soup and noodles were on special. All young rugby players with not a crust – consumable or otherwise – between us, we lived in abject poverty. Our flat needed furnishing, so we worked out a cunning plan – kerbside collection in the ritzy neighbourhoods.

Come collection day, we scoured the northern beaches' most affluent suburbs on the look out for half-decent furniture. And what we found was a bloody goldmine. To this day I don't think I've been able to purchase furniture as good as some of the stuff that was thrown out.

We picked up TVs – plural – with remotes and, more importantly, working batteries. We got hold of couches and knick-knacks and even beds. But it wasn't all flash.

One of the beds looked like it'd been utilised as a mating ground for three generations of gorilla. Better make that four 'cause I claimed that baby and made a nest out of it for many a night. In fact, I grew so fond of that mattress, it takes pride of place in my spare room to this very day… Not really. *Or does it?*

OUR FLAT NEEDED FURNISHING, SO WE WORKED OUT A CUNNING PLAN – KERBSIDE COLLECTION IN THE RITZY NEIGHBOURHOODS.

WORKING FOR THE MAN

Of course, as an amateur rugby player there's a lot of spare time on your hands. And I was lucky enough to find work with a bloke by the name of Carl McDonald, who ran a business making flashy signs for real estate agents. Like I mentioned earlier, I was no fan of manual labour and my attention span when it comes to things I don't

IT'S A DIFFICULT POSITION TO BE IN WHEN YOU'RE SO CLOSE TO YOUR DREAM IN ONE FIELD AND THEN SOMEONE'S SHIT-KICKER IN ANOTHER.

much care for makes even Millennials look focused. Suffice to say, I wasn't employee of the month.

It's a difficult position to be in when you're so close to your dream in one field and then someone's shit-kicker in another.

Lucky for me, Carl was a very tolerant human being. Though at times I'm certain he wanted to kill me, but held back. In saying that, there was the odd occasion when I thought about hammering him, too, but he was a tough little rooster and it could have gone either way.

I remember one day I was supposed to be working – apparently every day in the office is one of those days – and instead I was making planes from the corflute signs and launching them from

I REMEMBER ONE DAY I WAS SUPPOSED TO BE WORKING – APPARENTLY EVERY DAY IN THE OFFICE IS ONE OF THOSE DAYS

the warehouse roof. It would have been all right had the boss not caught me. And I probably could have kept my job had I not been yelling 'To infinity and beyond!' as it happened. It was pretty hard to explain it away as an accident.

Carl's face went redder than a bad rash, but lucky for me, we hit it off outside of work hours. He's a good bloke and turns out the reason he never knocked me out (apart from workplace health and safety rules that I don't think counted for much when it came to me) was because he wanted to manage me. And today, he remains my manager. And I can taunt him all I like without fear of getting bashed.

RACE FOR GLORY

It was the Olympic year and the only year in history prefaced with the word 'year' before the number – the year 2000, of course. And I was 13, about to take on the school running race called The St Francis Gift. And let me tell you, it wasn't the kind of gift most 13-year-olds are used to. No wrapping paper. Nothing. It was a 400 m dead straight, uphill slog. Come to think of it, the school must have been pinched for cash because the 'gift' was actually contested on a hot bitumen street connecting the main road to the back of the school. Nonetheless, it was a big event, with the whole school lining the entire track. 'Finally, the gauntlet of applause I've been dreaming of.'

IT WASN'T THE KIND OF GIFT MOST 13-YEAR-OLDS ARE USED TO. NO WRAPPING PAPER. NOTHING.

I was in the boys' division – years 8 to 12 – and not only were bragging rights and a Macca's voucher on the line, but the winner was going to get his name on the school honour board and get the coveted title as 'fastest kid in school'.

I WAS A COMPETITIVE LITTLE BUGGER AND BELIEVED I COULD PUT THE WIND UP A FEW OF THESE OLDER KIDS

Now, I'd only just turned 13. And I'd barely developed a stray underarm hair let alone the kind of brussels the Year 12 lads were parading about. But I was up for the challenge. Hopefully cut a few of the big Year 12 lads down and have my mates know I could outrun the seniors – an imperative and invaluable asset for a Year 8 battler. That's as good as being the bloke with the cigs in the prison yard – the guy who 'can get you things'.

Anyhow, a couple hundred lined up on the start line – aged 13 to 17. And before the start of the race I positioned myself at the front of the crowd against the strict commands of the teachers. I was a competitive little bugger and believed I could put the wind up a few of these older kids if I just had the chance. And hell, there was no way the teachers could catch me if they tried. So, there I was, standing at the front, shortest by a long shot – a Shetland in a thoroughbred race. And getting pushed around by the big kids who were all talking the strategy of 'not going hard early' and 'just keeping a medium pace'.

I'd taken a good ol'-fashioned police beating before the start gun had even gone off and ended up about five metres behind the start line – absorbed by the heaving mass of puberty.

Then, boom! We were off! And it was like Mick Hooper's hotel room after a win – absolute chaos as people were falling and getting trampled on just to get across the line. But I had my wits about me. This was like the dinner table rush in a family of eight. So I jumped over a couple then realised I had to get out of the traffic and strategically ran to the side of the pack and into the greenery beside the bitumen – through that soft mulch – and made up a heap of ground.

I might have reeked of eucalyptus but I'd managed to get myself right behind the leaders. At only 100 metres in, I cracked a smile – 'This is my time'. I knew their plan was to cruise early and then finish strong – a strategy I've implemented many times under the doona since. But then and there, I knew I had to act swiftly in the narrow window of opportunity I had.

So I accelerated with all my might and harder and longer than I'd ever done before. And it was working! With 50 metres to go I had a commanding lead. And the looks on the faces of the girls in my grade (which even under fatigue I couldn't help but notice) spoke of shock and awe at what they were seeing – a boy becoming a man in front of their very eyes. Spurred on, I pushed harder again. It was mine. But then with 30 to go things started slowing down rapidly – and not in a glorious slow-motion way either…

THEN WITH 30 TO GO THINGS STARTED SLOWING DOWN RAPIDLY

I turned to see where the rest were and spotted one bloke closing in fast as I began to get dizzier than a cat stuck in a dryer. I tried to kick again. No response. The lactic acid had taken over.

And with 10 to go, my eyesight blurred and swirling as the proverbial greyhound snapped at me heels, I even tried to run in the line he was taking to buy myself a metre. But with five to go my vision had deteriorated so badly that I could barely make out the finish line, which was marked out by two fluoro witches hats. I was delirious.

I got top heavy and as I tried to hold on for the win I began to stumble and fall forward. I put in one last step to dive head-first over the line – remembering we're on Brisbane's finest bitumen – as I passed out unconscious. I was like an Eskimo at the fair – out cold. And when I finally awoke some minutes later on the grass beside the finish line, I was lost. Couldn't move. My lower body had seized up from the lactic acid and my legs looked like literal

I WAS LIKE AN ESKIMO AT THE FAIR – OUT COLD.

greyhounds had in fact been snapping at my heels. They were a bloody mess.

I still didn't know the result. And as I was being carted to the sick bay a teacher walked up to me and said 'Great run, Nick' and handed me a medal. And this was before the days when 'participation medals' were handed out like flyers. I clenched it hard and opened one eye to see what colour it was… silver.

It was crushing defeat. If I wasn't already feeling sick I certainly was now. All for nothing. Never had **I CLENCHED IT HARD AND OPENED ONE EYE TO SEE WHAT COLOUR IT WAS... SILVER.** I felt like I deserved something more than that day.

But I sucked it up, cleaned the sickbay out of bandages and that stingy red fluid, and an hour later walked back to class bandaged like a mummy.

"MATE, WE'RE JUST MORE FOCUSED ON TREADING SOFTLY AND CARRYING A BIG STICK. "

TRANSLATION: 'We'll play it cool. Sneak up on the pricks real quiet and then smash 'em before they've even had a chance to know we were coming all along.'

TEST DEBUT

When I was about 17 years old, my old man told me he'd had a dream that I would score a try in a really important match. Possibly even a Test match.

Had he had a few beers? Sure. Did he often wake me up on a school night to tell me of his prophecies? You betcha. Did they ever come true? Rarely. But this dream was an exception for two reasons: One, it would come true. And two, it didn't feature Elle Macpherson.

Fast forward to 2011 and low and behold, I found myself in the Wallabies squad. And Dad was contemplating giving up the landscaping game and throwing up a 'Palms Read $5' sign out front of the house.

Anyhow, I was training for a month and every other bugger

was getting a run. But not me! Every injury brought me closer to a gig but still, I was down the line. And Dad's new-found psychic abilities weren't any help. He just kept telling me stuff I already knew.

Mentally, it was getting really difficult. We'd go to open training sessions and the public would come to meet their heroes. Kids lined up to get autographs but not mine. I was talking to a few of the boys and the mums were giving me the deadlies. 'Stop pushing in and give the kids a chance!' Nathan Sharpe, who played with me in Perth, started signing my jumper. Not even my own team-mate recognised me. OK, that's a lie, but that's how low I felt. The groundsman was getting more love than I was.

But the Perth Test was coming up soon and I thought surely I'll get a gig there, in front of my home crowd. But not this time either.

THE GROUNDSMAN WAS GETTING MORE LOVE THAN I WAS.

Now, I'd done tours with the Aussie Sevens but this was different. It was a Test match and I was mixing with the big boys now – even if they didn't recognise me.

It was a Tuesday I'll never forget when Robbie Deans pulled me aside and I prepared myself for the usual 'Your time will come'.

But as I walked towards him, he was grinning like a dead sheep – no Kiwi pun intended. And I just thought: 'Bugger you, Robbie. Don't crush my dreams again.' And then he said those three little words I'd been waiting to hear my whole life: 'Badge, you're in!'

I couldn't believe it. I just smiled. He's not such a bad bloke — for a Kiwi. A pretty good one, actually.

The phone rang at home. 'Hey, Dad. I've got you some Wallaby gear.'

He replied: 'Good stuff, mate. I appreciate that. It'll probably look better on me than you anyway.' Then I dropped the big one: 'And by the way, I'm starting for Australia on Saturday.' Dad: 'Mate! Do you want me to come over?' Me: 'Well, I can't do it on my own.' Dad: 'Right, mate. I'm in. But where the bloody hell are you?'

Rosario, Argentina, was the answer.

It's a reasonably big town of about one million people and they love their rugby. There is a moat around most of the ground separating the spectators from the field. And it's about five metres deep and three metres wide. Throw some water and barra in there and the place would be heaven.

Better yet, the crowd in Rosario cheer when anyone gets hammered and whip out the lasers when anyone has a shot at goal. Sport at its best!

The old man and my manager, Carl, flew out of Sydney on some airline which shall remain nameless. And by all reports, the flight was average at best. They had one movie which was in Spanish – with no nudity – but the language barrier didn't matter because the headphones didn't work anyway.

Surprise surprise, the old boy was pretty thirsty but there was no hostess to be seen.

In those situations Dad has always taught us that if someone won't help you, you help yourself. So with Dad as their leader, a group of no less than six men took turns at the bar stash. By the time the hostess had returned, the boys had drunk the bastard dry. And David Boon wasn't on this flight.

As a result, they went to sleep soundly but no one else on the plane could, as the snores echoed through the cabin to deafening effect. But with a good night's sleep under his belt, Dad's optimism was just what I needed when he arrived in camp.

Like a long-tailed cat in a room full of rocking chairs, I was pretty nervous.

There was a fair bit of tension because the team were under the pump in the media back home — Australia just had to win.

The jumper presentation was very humbling and the old bloke was proud as. I turned 25 next day before the game and Dad couldn't help but organise a cake and candles at a local restaurant – just to add some embarrassment to my nerves.

I found Dad a room with the only person who'd take him – Federico Pucciariello, a former Italian international front-rower. He was a big wheel in town who didn't speak all that much English – or at least could pretend he didn't – so I knew Dad wouldn't get under his skin, because all he kept harping on about was how he had a dream four years ago that I'd score a try for the Wallabies in a Test match. And his powers of prophecy were about to be put to the test…

Game Day

The captain's run was okay the day before but I was still a bit dodgy. I was rooming with big Kane Douglas and he was almost as untidy as me.

The place was a shambles – like my guts – and I could have forgiven the room service for contemplating self-harm. It was game day and I'd have given anything to curl up in that mess of a bed.

But this was my debut. My moment. And we grabbed our gear and onto the bus we went. And just quietly, the bus ride did little to calm my nerves.

The bloody thing roared through the town flat-out and the pedestrians just had to jump out of the way. The bus driver was Argentina's answer to Evel Knievel.

THE BUS DRIVER WAS ARGENTINA'S ANSWER TO EVEL KNIEVEL.

He was a mad bastard. I can't be certain, but I was sure he was drinking.

Finally, I'm on the field. Kitted up. And the national anthems were just a blur. I was so focused on not ballsing things up I don't think I sung a word of the Aussie anthem. But somehow knew the Argentinian anthem by heart. Was I a genius, after all?

The whistle finally went and it was more of a relief than anything. No more waiting.

The game itself was tough and while I didn't get many chances, I felt I did my job.

THE THINGS THEY SAID THEY'D DO TO OUR LIVESTOCK WERE SIMPLY APPALLING.

Our kickers did well coping with the lasers and I'd never heard so much heckling from a crowd. The things they said they'd do to our livestock were simply appalling. Joke's on them but, little did they know we had no livestock. Ha!

We survived the match – the local livestock, too – and when we won the old man convinced someone to give him a police escort onto the ground. He hugged me and just lost it. What a big moment!

Back in the changing room, Robbie Deans asked me and the old man to stand in the middle of the circle and lead the national anthem – the Australian one, not the Argentinian one.

It was a moment I'll always cherish. The whole thing was a buzz.

Dad's whole dream hadn't come true but a few years later I notched a match-winner against England and he wasted no time claiming he'd predicted the whole thing.

THE
RESCUE

I've been in need of my brothers' help more often than I'd like to admit – to them at least. Cocky bastards. But there's one incident I've got no shame in giving Nathan credit for.

We were on the way to Double Island Point – one of the best surf breaks on the east coast. Boards on, roosters in and we were away. Luckily as young kids, we all had shoulders like snakes and managed to fit into the truck.

Anyhow, we pulled up next to a massive hill up to a cliff that overlooked the beach and climbing that damn thing became priority No. 1. Surfing can wait. Boy, was that a mistake.

Why did we climb it? Because the bastard was there. That's been my philosophy for a lot of my extra-curricular triumphs over the years.

Anyhow, just after we'd made it to the summit, dragging our bare feet over crusty coral and rocks to get there, the old man called us down.

WHY DID WE CLIMB IT? BECAUSE THE BASTARD WAS THERE.

She was steep, and the only way to get down was flat-out or fall arse-over-head trying. So we knocked it into second and legged it.

I was racing Nathan and we were neck-and-neck – I could have been in front now I think about it. But Nath made it. And I didn't.

Some clown put a tree in the middle of my trajectory and I hit it at Mach 2. It was like being squirrel-gripped by Richie McCaw during a charity fun run. It made no sense. And it bloody well hurt. I fought the tears.

Nathan saw I'd virtually been impaled, and like a rat down a drainpipe he was there. He picked me up and carried me to the bottom. He was a strong bastard. But you think he's let me forget it? With skills like that, no wonder he's captain of the Norwegian rugby team.

DINGO DEADLOCK

It's 1998 and here I am, knob high to a ladybug – or 11 in proper English – and on a fishing adventure with the old man on Fraser Island.

Like any shagger with a penchant for fishing, we caught the barge from Inskip Point, just up the road from Rainbow Beach, to Fraser and while Dad was all about fishing, all I could think about were the dingoes and stories of attacks on kids. Odds on, I was next.

So we're in the truck driving along the beach, me on high dingo alert, and the old boy spots a gutter. 'Righto, so we're doing this. We're having a cast. No problem.' Until Dad decides to partake of a marathon walk along the beach trying different spots. What wasn't running through my mind? 'Has the old boy had enough?

Am I a sacrifice? Is this some sort of fishing ritual – give up a kid for a net full of dart?'

Anyhow, last thing I wanted was for Dad to think I was a pussy. Hell, I was 11 years old. Pretty much a man – bar the Adam's apple. So, not wanting to sound scared, I casually ask him: 'Dad, you reckon we should bring the knife along? You know, just in case?' He obliges. Thinks nothing more of it. I wasn't going down without a fight.

So a little while later Dad's about 200 metres up the beach, I'm casting my lure and then I start getting the feeling I'm being watched. A feeling I'm quite accustomed to these days… Anyhow, I look around but there's nothing. But this feeling won't go away. Like a Melbourne Cup hangover, it just becomes stronger and stronger. So I do my best impersonation of Michael Jackson, spin around on me heels and suddenly, there it is – a bloody dingo, standing at the tree line 40 metres away with its eyes right on me! It was a specimen-size build and healthy. If anything, abnormally large. Record-breaking even.

THERE IT IS – A BLOODY DINGO, STANDING AT THE TREE LINE 40 METRES AWAY WITH ITS EYES RIGHT ON ME!

I surmise he's too far away to do anything with the knife. I mean, I was confident I could throw it that far and hit him between the eyes. What 11-year-old wouldn't be? But I had a whiting on the other line. So I tried to be calm about it so as not to encourage an attack – or worse, incite one and it be my fault.

By this time, Dad was too far up the beach to hear me and the car was further away than the dingo. I was like a

I WAS LIKE A BASEBALL PLAYER CAUGHT BETWEEN BASES – ONLY THE CONSEQUENCES WERE LETHAL.

baseball player caught between bases – only the consequences were lethal. So I took a leaf out of the book of the girls from school I liked looking at and just turned away, pretending not to care. (They cared…)

I kept fishing, thoughts of Dad crying 'A dingo stole my Nicky' running through my head. I checked again and it has narrowed the gap. It was now 30 metres and stationary. Then 20 metres and still crouched, nose pointing directly at me in a stalk position. This dingo must have thought it was a forest frog because it was doing its best to camouflage itself.

Now, my heart is pounding as I slowly unclip the button on the knife sheath and readied myself for battle. I'd seen *Gladiator* on Channel 7. This was classic one-on-one stuff. Then I remembered a story my cousin Ben told me about how a kangaroo survived a pack of hunting dogs by leading the dogs to a dam and then taking up position in the middle. When the dogs came in swimming after the kangaroo he pushed them down and held them under the water until they were motionless. 'Bloody genius, kangaroo!' I thought. 'No wonder you're on the national coat of arms.' But I also understood the dingo's plight. Kangaroo ain't a bad feed.

I STARTED YELLING AT IT, BUT ITS EYES MEANT BUSINESS. I WAS A GONER.

Anyhow, with that knowledge fresh in my head I began backing up towards the water with the rod held out in front of me and the knife at the ready. My plan was to let it bite the rod – minds out of the gutter, people – while I tried to stab the eyes. Like my worst nightmare, it began following me into the water.

I started yelling at it, but its eyes meant business. I was a goner. And as I swung my rod around wildly – again, gutters people – Dad comes roaring around the corner and yells the six words that somehow scare off animals and men of all size – 'GET OUT OF IT YA BASTARD!' And a few more expletive terms that I'm certain the dingo didn't understand, though Dad insists it did.

And sure enough, the dingo retreated back to the tree line. And I haven't been to Fraser or fished on a beach since.

KABOOM IN CAMBODIA

I'm no stranger to taking things into my own hands when a job needs to be done. Get your heads out of the gutter. So while touring solo through Cambodia, and having heard whispers in the hostel of a secret location rife with live World War II weapons you can shoot, I ventured out to find out for myself.

I arrived at an army installation and met with a major of the Cambodian Army – he looked about 12. Anyhow, he brought a folder out with pictures of different weapons that I could choose to fire. A veritable smorgasbord of 1944's most technologically advanced weaponry. I turned down the combo offer of a Browning machine gun and rocket launcher with live cow. Apparently, this is a popular option where if you miss the cow with the rocket launcher, you take it out with a high-calibre machine gun.

Sensing the magnitude of the karmic backlash associated with such an act, I respectfully declined. It would be a poor way to honour one of nature's greatest beasts. Plus, it would be a waste of steak.

I had my mind set on the rocket-propelled

I TURNED DOWN THE COMBO OFFER OF A BROWNING MACHINE GUN AND ROCKET LAUNCHER WITH LIVE COW.

grenade. I asked how much and he replied: '$200' in very broken English. I thought that was steep, so I tried to negotiate a better price – with a weapons dealer...

The major quickly turned aggressive and began shouting in Cambodian. Lucky for me, I'd spent some time in Matraville and picked up a little lingo. From what I could surmise it was just friendly banter. That was until the major stormed off in search of ammo and an elderly American tourist approached me with heavy caution: 'You're in a third world country, I strongly suggest you accept his offer'. Strewth! I shit myself. And quickly began to realise I could have just dug my own grave. Actually, I hadn't been asked to dig my own grave yet so I still had time to put on some of that classic Cummins charm.

So the major returns, I throw cash at him like he's a stripper and give him a huge grin. He reciprocates. Almost menacingly. And we set off on a two-hour drive on some outback tracks – presumably for me to dig my own grave. We finally pull up at an old hut. The major gets out of the car, goes inside and comes out with an AK47 alongside another soldier. My heart sinks. 'This is it, Cummo. You're like a palm tree in a cyclone – rooted.'

MY HEART SINKS. 'THIS IS IT, CUMMO. YOU'RE LIKE A PALM TREE IN A CYCLONE – ROOTED.'

So through my best efforts of body language I try to express to the major that I did not ask for the gun he was carrying. He ignores me. And now they both get in the car and we proceed along rough windy tracks for half an hour.

We come to a halt, my heart still pounding as I think to myself: 'No one will ever know I was here. The world will never get to know the real me. The Badger.'

The major picks up the AK47 from the boot and walks around to my door, holding the gun at hip height. He then proceeds to point the gun at me and use it to wave me out of the car. Like a virgin prom queen, I refused his advances. This was gonna be the end of me.

And if he didn't take kindly to bartering you can only imagine how he reacted to flat-out rejection. So he grew frustrated and made bigger movements with the gun. I thought to myself: 'My only chance is to go along with his demands until I see an opportunity to disarm and disable the major and the soldier'. This was Van Damme stuff.

So I get out and follow him around behind some bushes, being sure to be close enough behind to take the major to ground before he can fire. I look over my shoulder and realise it's just the two of us. 'This is my shot'.

I'm waiting for any sudden movement from him to make my move. I'm about to tackle him when he takes his hand off the trigger, which puts me on stand-by. He turns to see me in his sky rocket (pocket), which gives him a fright. Then, holding only the barrel, he hands me the gun and says: 'Two shot to mountain'. I hastily accept the weapon. Not knowing why he is handing it to me, he explains: 'Two shot so people hide'. Not fully understanding what he meant, and without delay, I shot two rounds over the mountains, just in case.

I then swap the AK47 for the Russian-made RPG. I throw it over my shoulder and assume firing position. The major squats down beside me and initiates countdown. Then a massive plume of smoke shot out behind me as the rocket accelerated and exploded into the mountain. Crisis averted.

On the trip back, the major explained that the mountain I was shooting towards is actually populated. 'Shit!' But that the two shots were to warn them that a rocket is headed their way.

It really is a solo traveller's paradise…

THE NEW BOY SNAPS A HAMSTRING

What a year 2008 was about to be. From a relative unknown trudging the brown grass of Bundaberg to Western Force Super Rugby. Things were looking up for one Nick F. Cummins. And like a hippie with a dole cheque, I strutted into day one of the pre-season with a real groove in my step. 'What a day for it!'

Anyhow, the strength and conditioning coach thought it would be a good idea to kick off the very first day after the Chrissy holidays with speed testing over forty metres. Genius.

The speed gates were set up in the basketball court and the players were instructed to do some run-throughs to warm up for the test. However, Cummo, the

I STRUTTED INTO DAY ONE OF THE PRE-SEASON WITH A REAL GROOVE IN MY STEP.

young bull (yeah, that's third person. It's my book. No rules.) was a little too eager to impress the head coach, John Mitchell.

Ten minutes goes by of warm-up and I've done more run-throughs than a rabbit in breeding season. And by the time it was

BY THE TIME IT WAS MY TURN FOR THE REAL TEST, YOU COULD PLAY A NOTE OFF MY HAMSTRINGS

my turn for the real test, you could play a note off my hamstrings – they were that tight. I'd either become a Guinness World Record holder on day one or an early casualty. Suffice to say, it was the latter.

At about the 35-metre mark, what felt like a sniper's bullet hit me direct in the right hamburglar. I went down like Pamela Anderson at the Playboy Mansion. It was brutal. And in an instant I was grimacing (get it?). Turned out to be a 14-centimetre tear and a five-week stint in rehab. Who was the genius now?

This was my first injury as a professional sportsman. Basically the equivalent of being suspended at school – a holiday, if you will.

So the next day I turned up to the field session in my best double pluggers keen to impress the coach. But ol' Johnny Mitchell didn't take too kindly – said that I was taking the piss and gave me the kind of spray usually reserved for the parking inspector.

And there's a lesson to be learned from all this, kids. Never rock up to work with the wrong footwear.

MAKING A MEAL OF IT

To say I like my tucker is akin to saying rabbits don't mind a shag. Please. They're mating maniacs. And I'd jump on a Mardi Gras float for a sniff of a good steak. Beef, of course.

I'D JUMP ON A MARDI GRAS FLOAT FOR A SNIFF OF A GOOD STEAK.

So when it was suggested I undertake a course to accompany my training, my first question was, 'How many courses? Entree and dessert?' Alas, they meant an 'adult learning' course. And a business certificate at that.

It's a rugby thing. Each year a few players sign up to do courses and certificates to serve them in the future. It's a great initiative. And I expect it will serve me well someday.

However, for a bloke who struggled with attention in 6th grade, the term 'study' didn't exactly incite fits of rapture. But no sooner had I attended my first lesson than I abruptly changed my tune. Like I had been struck by lightning or touched by angels – *appropriately* – I found a new love for study… (coughs) Bullshit. Turns out, the old college put on quite the spread for the business students. The sangers were outstanding and numerous. And this outweighed the pain of the drawn-out lessons.

Perhaps the teacher knew Sam Wykes and myself were one bad prawn cocktail away from pulling the plug, because he upped the smorgasbord weekly to match the ascending difficulty of the class. Each white bread delicacy more satisfying than the last.

That made it extremely difficult for Sammy and myself to leave. When you're on the bones of your arse, opportunities to fill your guts with some good tucker must be taken seriously. Even if it meant going against everything you stand for and getting smarter in the process…

WHEN YOU'RE ON THE BONES OF YOUR ARSE, OPPORTUNITIES TO FILL YOUR GUTS WITH SOME GOOD TUCKER MUST BE TAKEN SERIOUSLY.

So despite having to sit through talks twice a week that would put an accountant to sleep, we hung in there. Coupled with the freshest juices in town, the joint was basically offering high tea for the price of a waiting room water. Needless to say, we entered each meeting with no less than six empty pockets each. I'm still picking out glazed salmon tart from my lucky trousers – which in hindsight, aren't as lucky as they are stinky. When it came time to hand in our end-of-season assignments, the brains quickly realised we had no clue what we were talking about. And CCTV footage revealed

I'M STILL PICKING OUT GLAZED SALMON TART FROM MY LUCKY TROUSERS

we were only there for the meal. I can only imagine it was like watching a wildlife documentary in infrared vision, with two hyenas sneakily picking at a zebra carcass and coming back for more. And more. And more…

"I'M AS FULL AS A CENTRELINK ON PAYDAY. "

TRANSLATION: 'Due to political forces and the economic climate, many Australians have taken a hit in the hip pocket and forced into unemployment. As such, many have little choice but to enrol in government-funded payments and are eager to collect said payments every second Friday. And the place gets full.'

WATER BIRTH

In my first season of Super Rugby, we were playing a Kiwi team at Patterson Stadium in Subiaco, Perth.

We were attempting to run it out from our 22 and the ball came to me. You beauty! I jigged, stepped, half got around their winger but he was hanging onto my jersey. I continued to pump the legs like a Warner Bros. cartoon character and manage to stay stationary at the same time – quite the feat – until he landed smack on the back of my ankle with an all-mighty crack!

The play moved on, but I couldn't move. The physio arrived and in no uncertain terms told me to quit being a little bitch: 'Get up, you're fine', the physio said. And why wouldn't I listen to the physio? I'm no doctor.

So I rolled over to my stomach to take a good look back at my ankle – which right on cue fell to the side diagonally from my leg.

I was carried from the field with a broken fibula and syndesmosis with a six-month recovery ahead of me. But it didn't end there. I was rushed in for surgery. The nurse dressed me for theatre and said: 'Take this tablet. It will make you drowsy'. But I'd seen the ads. Last thing I was gonna do was take a pill from a complete stranger. Was she trying to take advantage of me? Hell, it wouldn't have surprised me. Anyhow, turns out it was standard protocol. So I dropped it in and then waited for the call. When I rolled into theatre the anaesthetist gave me the first hit of anaesthetic and told me I'd be out in five minutes. Ten minutes goes by and I'm not the slightest bit sleepy. I was on high alert. And as I looked up from the operating table, I could see four heads with full surgical kits hovering over me, waiting for me to go under. At this point I was dead-set shitting myself because I thought I was about to feel everything. Hell, they were on a schedule. I yelled out. 'Hey, doc! I'm not out yet, mate! Put away the knife!' So the doc looks at his watch and then tells the anaesthetist to whack in another dose. You beauty!

She's puzzled, but agrees. I'd seen that puzzled look on a woman's face before. And trust me, it's not good. It normally finishes with the words: 'Let's just forget the whole thing'. But in this case, I didn't want to be in a state to remember anything in the first place.

So I stop her. 'You reckon this one will work, doc?' The doc: 'You'll be gone in 10 seconds'. So I say: 'Righto, smartarse. Let's have a bet – if I can make fourteen seconds, you owe me 10 bucks – deal? I'll see it on my chest when I wake up. If I don't, I owe you five bucks.' He agrees. Admittedly, somewhat reluctantly.

The anaesthetist gives me another hit and we start the clock. Being cocky, and thinking I was invincible, I confidently counted, as my vision blurred, all the way to sixteen before going under. When I woke up I looked for the Chris McKenna. Hell, just thinking about the food I could buy with $10 got me through the operation. Couldn't die then and there from complicated ankle surgery. But get this, the tight bastard didn't pay his debt. He sent me home with some painkillers, stressing the importance of hydration while on this medication. If the old man taught me one thing, it's you can't trust a man who doesn't pay his

IF THE OLD MAN TAUGHT ME ONE THING, IT'S YOU CAN'T TRUST A MAN WHO DOESN'T PAY HIS DEBTS.

debts. So I wasn't about to be fooled into taking his 'professional' advice. So I fobbed it off and said: 'She'll be right, mate'.

This is where it gets gross.

So, a week goes by and I realise I haven't snapped one off in a while. I made an embarrassing trip to the chemist and using the most delicate term I could conjure, inquired about some 'constipation-busters' for a 'friend' that's in strife at the moment. But after two days of pills, still nothing.

So I decided to pull up stumps on the old Gary Glitter to initiate movement. I'd read about Caesar and how he dealt with the problem – rolling on his stomach and having his servants pick it out. Well, the boys weren't down for that and Mum never replied to the text.

I REMEMBERED MY SISTERS TALKING ABOUT WATER BIRTHS. 'CUMMO, YOU GENIUS.'

So I took it upon myself to do something about it. An hour on the throne saw no progress but I remembered my sisters talking about water births. 'Cummo, you genius.'

So sheepishly, I relocated to the shower. And began grunting. Without too much detail, 30 minutes and two cracked shower tiles later I'd dropped 4 kilograms on the scales. And the only costs I incurred were the pills and bobcat hire for removal of the evidence.

Of course, it all could have been avoided had the stingy doc come good on his debt. I'd never have had to turn down his advice.

WHEELY-BIN BREAK-IN

While playing for Randwick, I was put up in Coogee near the rugby club with an old bloke going by the name Wayne. I suspect it was an alias but you never really can know for sure.

Anyhow, Wayno was in his late 50s, smoked like an '85 Barina and loved a good yarn almost as much as a punt. But boy did he get filthy if you woke him up. Which ordinarily wouldn't be a problem, only that he went to bed at 7 pm and left for work at 3:30 am. Now, my body clock was a tad different to ol' Wayno's and recently having been given the hard word, I decided to attempt an unorthodox second-storey *Mission Impossible* entry. And like T. Cruise himself, this one involved me doing all my own stunts which, in this case, meant the strategic placing of two wheely-bins on top of one another.

When the coast was clear and no cars in sight, I climbed from the neighbour's ground floor windowsill onto the second bin. Then I made the leap of faith from bin number two to my window – which, of course, was closed. Farking, Wayne! But with a cliffhanger-style manoeuvre I was able to open the window and pull myself in, landing on my bed with a perfect 10 and not moving until the next afternoon. Not a bad effort given I'd had a couple under the belt.

Of course, the Neighbourhood Watch lady living below us didn't see it that way and had no problem getting on the line to Wayno when she found the wheely-bins stacked by her window along with some remnants of a doner kebab.

Wayne wasn't stoked – to say the least. But what that man wouldn't forgive for a carton of Toohey's finest… Asking him to move his car at 9 pm is what.

It's shift work, but someone's gotta do it.

RICE
EXPERIMENT

Living in Kingsford, Sydney, is the equivalent of sleeping with someone below your standards. You gotta kiss a few toads before you find a princess. And upon moving to Sydney and at the whim of Randwick, I had little choice in my accommodations. But hey, any hole's a goal. And this place was a hole.

IT WAS THE HARDEST TIME OF MY LIFE – AWAY FROM HOME FOR THE FIRST TIME, AND HUNGRIER THAN KYLE SANDILANDS.

I had recently moved from Brisbane and was out of home for the first time. My experience in the real world amounted to zero times f*&k all – especially in a busy joint like Sydney.

I was doing my training with Carl McDonald, the most feared conditioning trainer in the land – and my boss at the time. Never

I WAS ALONE. BROKE. IN A NEW CITY AND HUNGRY ENOUGH TO EAT KYLE SANDILANDS.

having paid for grub before, I was quick to discover that 90 per cent of the money I earned was spent on food. It was the hardest time of my life – away from home for the first time, and hungrier than Kyle Sandilands.

This one particular day I was bloody cooked after three training sessions and a full day of work. So I ducked into an ATM for a quick $20 only to be greeted with arguably the most soul-destroying four words known to modern man – 'Transaction declined. Insufficient funds'.

Now, the best thing to do in these situations is panic. So I did just that and forked out another $2 of my hard-earned to check my balance. And if I was shattered before I was absolutely gutted when the figure $3.65 appeared on my screen. I was alone. Broke. In a new city and hungry enough to eat Kyle Sandilands.

So I began to think primal. I got home and was so tired and drained that I needed to eat within two minutes or I would pass out. I opened the cupboard. Damn it! I only had 3-minute noodles. That wouldn't suffice.

Then a lightbulb moment. I grabbed a coffee mug, jammed it full of rice and added some water. 'Nick, you genius. You've done it again.' And like that I chugged it down, confident it would expand in my stomach. 'Why has no one else thought of this?'

But it went down rougher than a Kiwi scrum, scratching my throat the whole way. I stumbled to my bed without showering or anything.

The next thing I remember is waking up late the next day, still in my rugby gear from the night before and scurrying off to training – but not before another hardy glass of rice. Some say rice milk was invented that very day. In that very room…

By the time I got to work my guts were making all kinds of noises. Then after a wind episode I felt something hit me undies. So I scurried to the dunny to check the dacks and was met with instant relief and amazement at the same time. It was a handful of completely intact rice grains, like they'd just been packed by Uncle Ben himself. Confused, I sat on the bowl to digest – pun intended – what had just happened and in no time silence turned to the sound of gravel being poured down a drain. It all looked reusable. But was it? Only one way to find out…

" ... ABOUT AS STRAIGHT AS A MARDI GRAS. "

TRANSLATION: 'The Sydney Gay and Lesbian Mardi Gras is a celebration of sexuality, freedom and life. People who find the opposite sex attractive are considered "straight" in slang terminology. Therefore, those who find the same sex attractive are considered to be the opposite of straight – round, maybe?'

SPIDER BITE!

One morning I woke up to an itch or bite, which was understandable given my mattress was off the street. I'd gotten used to the odd tick or louse so I took off to training without a care in the world, thankful the bite was mid thigh and not upper if you catch my drift…

I pulled through the session no worries and headed to work like always. But by the arvo I was starting to drag my arse around and my boss at the time – the now infamous Carl McDonald – was old school and as hard-arse as they come. You could show up with a broken arm and he'd tell you you're a pussy and to get on with it. And I didn't want it to

HE PROCEEDED TO TELL ME TO HARDEN UP AND STOP CARRYING ON. I COULDN'T WIN.

seem like I was trying to get out of any training because of a little bite. So when he asked, 'You 'right?', I said 'Yeah, she'll be right' and he proceeded to tell me to harden up and stop carrying on. I couldn't win.

So I finished work and went off to afternoon training hoping a good work-out would get whatever it was outta my system. Note to self: training when sick only exacerbates illness.

By the next morning I was in more shit than a Werribee duck. I couldn't eat – the official sign something was wrong – and was achieving less on the job than a council worker.

BY THE NEXT MORNING I WAS IN MORE SHIT THAN A WERRIBEE DUCK.

The manager became concerned when he saw the bite on my thigh and when he called the boss down I couldn't hide anything. I told him I was gonna see a doc and call him after. Then I showed him the huge rash, the swelling, the building pus and he shook his head: 'There's nothing bloody wrong with ya'. Thanks, doc.

So now I'm sitting in the waiting room at the surgery and was slipping in and out of focus. The doc asks me to sit on the bed and I struggled to bend my leg to sit up, as the infection had spread covering most of my quad and marching towards the Jatz Crackers.

Doc: 'Wow! How did you get here? You didn't drive?' I flashed him my car keys: 'Does this answer your question?'

He was more concerned than filthy and said he was surprised

I climbed the stairs to his office, let alone drove there. He said I'd been bitten by a poisonous spider and

THE INFECTION HAD SPREAD COVERING MOST OF MY QUAD AND MARCHING TOWARDS THE JATZ CRACKERS.

that as a result my glands were all swollen and the poison was moving through my bloodstream. 'Speak English, doc! I ain't no scientist!'

He then proceeded to lance the bite to allow pus to run out and insisted I start on two courses of medication immediately. He gave me the pills then and there before rattling off the dosage, which I can't say I was listening to.

He then sent me to hospital for overnight observation and said to call someone to pick me up and take me there. Who was I gonna call? Sure as shit not Carl. If he had his way he'd have had me back on the job and called me Nicole for the rest of my tenure. So I pretended to call someone for a lift as I walked out, then drove myself to the hospital.

But I could barely afford the petty cash to get there let alone hospital costs. And when that dawned on me, I hit the brakes quick smart and headed for home. Next thing, I was in a 60 zone and I could hear somebody huffing and puffing next to the car. I looked in my side mirror and this person arrived at my window asking where Woolies was. I looked down and the speedo said 60 km/h. Shocked and still looking at the speedo, I said: 'Geez, you're quick!' And when I turned again he was gone.

IT'S THEN I REALISED I WAS IN REAL STRIFE.

Whether he was even there in the first place was a big concern. Was I hallucinating? Or did I just encounter a UFO? Either way, it was then I realised I was in real strife. And just as I parked up out the back of the dungeon (unit), my world began to darken. And fearful of passing out in that dodgy area – where my ute had a brick thrown through the window three weeks earlier – I wound up my windows and locked my doors.

My strength suddenly disappeared and I saw the passenger door wasn't locked. So as I fell on my side I flicked the lock across as my head hit the passenger door and passed out.

A magpie woke me in the morning scratching around on the bonnet and looking at me.

I remember thinking something or someone must have been watching over me and protecting me that night. Most likely the homeless dude who made a bed in my tray.

But I was alive and strong enough to have a shower and head off to training. Pretty stupid really. I continued the medication but stopped two weeks early 'cause I was back on the burst, baby!

DROWNING WITH THE SHARKS

South Africa, 2015. The great white and tiger shark capital of the world. Just ask that bloody legend Mick Fanning, who fought one of the beasts bare-handed and lived to tell the tale. I hear the two are actually quite close now. The best friendships often begin with a scrap…

Jokes aside, a year earlier on tour in Durban I'd taken the opportunity to go cage diving with great whites. And it was a tops experience. But now I wanted more action.

So about an hour's drive from Durban I took on the shark diving all over again but this time, minus the cage.

Myself and some other fools boarded a scuba-diving boat that took us out through the surf break, which was an experience in itself, and then on to a spot where dolphins and turtles were cutting around. After a rapid 'safety' briefing that was about as informative as a Spanish infomercial in Dubbo, we were ready to hit the water. And by ready I mean shit-scared. Because our guide had scars from his armpit to the bottom of his ribs, which he informed us was where he was chomped by a shark while loading the burley bucket under the water with dead fish. You beauty!? All of a sudden a shark attack at a surf contest doesn't seem like such an anomaly. They're feeding the bastards over there!

Nathan Charles was on the surface holding on to a floating device with his head in the water. And he had that 'I'm probably going to die' look on his dial. The floaties certainly didn't give me a boost of confidence.

This also happened to be my first scuba dive. And if you haven't gathered already, paying attention has never been a strong point of mine. So once the instructor was done talking I just flicked myself overboard and started to sink to the bait bucket – and then beyond! And it wasn't on purpose. Turns out I was pressing the wrong button and was descending rapidly, equalising every few seconds.

IF YOU HAVEN'T GATHERED ALREADY, PAYING ATTENTION HAS NEVER BEEN A STRONG POINT OF MINE.

I started to panic, frantically pressing the other button and trying to unclip the weight belt. But it was difficult. I looked up from the darkness to see tiny humans bobbing on the surface and below me total darkness, with that feeling of something watching me.

I slowed down and then slowly began to rise. And just before I

I HEADBUTTED IT IN THE MOUTH AND ALL I COULD SEE WAS TEETH!

breached, a two-metre blacktip shark swam above me.

But I was still trying to shake the weight belt and without seeing the thing until the last second, I headbutted it in the mouth and all I could see was teeth!

With my heart rate reaching 600rpm, I was outta that water quicker than Nathan Charles could book himself swimming lessons and happy to give someone else a turn.

So there you have it, Mick Fanning wasn't the only Australian athlete to take on a shark and win in 2015. And I'm extremely glad we both lived to tell the tale – though mine is more one of stupidity and dumb luck while Mick's is all courage.

Aussies 2: South Africa 0.

ON FANS DRESSING UP LIKE HIM:

"I FIRST OF ALL THOUGHT 'WHAT THE HELL IS WRONG WITH THAT BASTARD?' THEN I REALISED, JESUS, THEY WERE BEING ME."

TRANSLATION: 'It's an absolute honour to be considered a god in people's eyes and each and every one of them is a dead set hot genius. Support our troops.'

TROUBLE IN DUBLIN

The 2013 Wallabies Spring Tour was a buzz. Three out of four wins against the European powerhouses was a pretty good result for me. Sadly, my work off the field wasn't as sharp.

It started innocently enough. The night out in Ireland on the Tuesday before the Test was huge. And so was the match suspension I got as a result…

We all went out to dinner through the week before the Test. And all was going well until we were invited to a nightclub. Hell yeah, I'm in!

The cabs turned up at the Temple Bar and we filed into them like a well oiled machine. We

THREE OUT OF FOUR WINS AGAINST THE EUROPEAN POWERHOUSES WAS A PRETTY GOOD RESULT FOR ME.

THE MUSIC WAS ON, THE BLOKES WERE PRIMED AND WE HAD THE ROOM TO OURSELVES.

stumbled out later, like circus clowns. The short journey was uneventful in itself, but we were about to make up for it.

We jumped the queue – one of the perks of being a 'big deal' – and roared up the stairs. The music was on, the blokes were primed and we had the room to ourselves. What's wrong with this picture? NO sheilas is what. Not a bloody bird in the room. If I wanted to spend my time with 20 sweaty blokes I'd join a rugby team. And seeing as though I'd already done that, I wasn't too keen on the lack of babes.

Luckily, I've got a bit of halfback in me and I had a red-hot thought. So I ran to the bartender and said, 'Mate, send up every good sort in the line outside for the backs. And the rest for the forwards. And no more blokes!'

I RAN TO THE BARTENDER AND SAID, 'MATE, SEND UP EVERY GOOD SORT IN THE LINE OUTSIDE FOR THE BACKS. AND THE REST FOR THE FORWARDS.'

This is a classic nightclub quandary. Guys wanna go where the girls are. But the girls wanna go where they can be left alone. It was a good ol'-fashioned sausage fest and I wasn't having none of it.

So up the stairs the girls came, surging their way into Australian rugby folklore without even knowing it. Hell, we didn't know it at the time.

Big, small, winners and grinners; the unattached men of the Australian rugby team made a beeline for the girls with tales of leather-bound books and mahogany dressing rooms. And the girls loved it. They genuinely love rugby in Ireland and even the forwards get a look in.

But there was one particular bloke who stood out more than most. The leader of the pack. The rascal. The ring leader. The bad influence… My old man, Mark. And he'd be in anything.

He couldn't believe what he was seeing. He sat there and just absorbed the occasion, thinking to himself: 'How long has this been going on and why haven't I been a part of it?' Simple answer, Dad: you're rubbish at footy. But he did make the team of the century.

One of the lads, who will remain nameless but wears a number higher than 10 and less than 15, asked Dad if he wanted to meet a woman. Apparently a few of the girls' grandmothers were at a local knitting circle around the corner. But, like the gentleman and/or creep he is – you decide – he declined and said he was happy just to watch.

APPARENTLY A FEW OF THE GIRLS' GRANDMOTHERS WERE AT A LOCAL KNITTING CIRCLE AROUND THE CORNER.

Next thing we know, a sort walks straight to the old boy and introduces herself. She was keen. Touching and flirting. There were only two possibilities – she'd spiked her own drink or one of the lads had put her up to it.

Nope. Wrong. Just as Dad was hitting his stride and the attention of the team had turned to this no-name shagger who

THE OLD MAN'S NOGGIN LOOKS AS IF IT'S BEEN PUT TOGETHER LIKE A RANSOM NOTE

seemingly has a silver tongue, we heard the seven best words to ever come from a bird's mouth – or the seven most demoralising if you're my old man. She says: 'You look different on TV, Mr McKenzie'. Second thought, the old man's noggin looks as if it's been put together like a ransom note, so Ewen has the right to be the most pissed.

Before the team had even had a chance to crack up in laughter, Dad gave me that 'you big bastard' look, knowing I'd set him up, but continued with the charade until he was ready to hit the road.

Truth is, he was more red than a tradie's porn collection and bailed down the stairs, only for one of the boys to grab him in a headlock, load him up with a couple of shots and suitcase him into a cab before he'd even had a chance to ponder what had just happened.

The rest of us followed suit a few minutes later and returned home undamaged and ready to get back into training after blowing off some steam.

SEVEN OF US HAD BEEN SUSPENDED FOR ONE MATCH FOR GOING OUT AND HAVING A FEW HARMLESS DRINKS.

However, we woke up to be welcomed by ARU hierarchy and the news that seven of us had been suspended for one match for going out and having a few harmless drinks. No one had gotten into any trouble the night before or done anything untoward. Not a single complaint. Except from the broad who thought she'd met Ewen McKenzie only to realise it was just a landscaper from Brisbane.

Or maybe it wasn't Dad and it was in fact Ewen? At least that would explain how we ended up in trouble…

Regardless, it was a top night and one I'll remember – and be reminded of – for years to come.

" YOU GET ONE OPPORTUNITY. YOU BALLS IT UP AND YOU ARE IN STRIFE. "

TRANSLATION: 'I stole that one from the girl I lost my virginity to. Basically, don't f*&k it up or I'll make sure you suffer either physical or mental consequences.'

SHARK BAIT

If the dingoes and centipedes don't get ya up Rainbow/Fraser way, then the sharks are sure as shit willing to pick up the slack. Queensland beaches are deadlier than a rhino on a dance floor but that never stopped Dad from putting us in harm's way. Or our willingness to test ourselves against the most dangerous elements nature had to offer. Hell, as a young boy, it's a rite of passage to dice with death and laugh in the face of a friend or sibling

QUEENSLAND BEACHES ARE DEADLIER THAN A RHINO ON A DANCE FLOOR

who was stupid enough to suffer the fate you evaded.

Anyhow, we were fishing along the beach as we often did and scouring the great white sands for a good fishing spot – you know, a deep channel inside a sandbank. Take note amateurs, that's Good Fishing 101.

Problem is, like most forward packs, them sharks aren't as dumb as they look. And as we pulled up to our secret gutter we discovered the tiger sharks had beaten us to it. The good news was, they were chasing the bait fish onto the shore. You beauty! The better news was, I had just been given the opportunity to fulfil my life-long dream of catching a shark. You ripper! So I grabbed the rods from the truck and took the buggers on. Armed with me river rod, 130 lb line and an egg beater – sans trace – what could possibly go wrong? Right? And just quietly, it wasn't the first time an Ugly Stik was passed around our camp…

So I threw down the challenge to the old man, baited up the flathead hook with some fresh bait fish hand-caught by yours truly and cast in the line ready to taste victory. I could already see my photo in the *Sunshine Coast Daily*, a little feature on *Brownie's Coastwatch*; perhaps I'd even take a call from Rex Hunt and the crew. Prob'ly even get some sort of sponsorship offer and no doubt, as toast of the town, some of its best women.

A few minutes in and all was going to plan. I'd hooked one and the old boy had been snapped off – it was my beach now, codger. Being in command of a light rod has become second nature nowadays – wink wink – but back then, I'd never experienced such power between my legs. And for me, gutter language meant one thing – fishing. Get it?

Anyhow, the tiger shark was mine. Craig, I named him – a Christian name that exemplifies a cunning bastard hiding in plain sight. He might look bland, but throw a hook at him – right, left, fish or otherwise – and he'll sure as shit put up a fight. And that ol' Craig did. I battled him from

THE LOCAL KIDS CAME RUNNING. STARTED CHANTING NAMES LIKE 'MERLIN' AND 'NEPTUNE'.

the beach, by twig arm and egg-beater doing my choice of attire – singlet – proud. I was king of the ocean. The local kids came running. Started chanting names like 'Merlin' and 'Neptune'.

And like that little annoying c-word (crustacean) I fought until the bitter end when ol' Craig had had his fill – I reckon he must have had at least 27 mouthfuls of other bait fish while he was on the line – and said 'See ya, wanker', snapped my line and took off like the cunning bastard I always knew he was.

We only knew each other a short time. A moment, if you will. But every time a wave breaks on the shore, it whispers 'Craiiiggg'.

ON BEING CALLED THE HONEY BUDGER IN A JAPANESE MAGAZINE:

" THE JOURNO WAS CONFUSED AS A GOLDFISH WITH DEMENTIA. "

TRANSLATION: 'Goldfish are renowned for having short memories that last no longer than three seconds. Which is why you can't believe that movie *Finding Nemo* – it was founded on lies. Dementia is a mental disease that corrodes the brain and results in sufferers losing many physical and mental abilities – namely, their memories. Therefore, a goldfish with dementia would be massively confused.'

RODEO MOON

Having schoolteachers as parents afforded our family the ability to enjoy 10 weeks holiday a year – to spend every school holidays together. And if you haven't gathered already – firstly, please see a doctor – we spent most of that time at Rainbow Beach.

And there were few more exciting occasions in town than the annual rodeo. With no shortage of sand, they'd gather up 50-odd tonne of the stuff and dump it in the pub car park. It worked on every level. Right by the beer for the adults, plenty of pink lemonade for the kids and close enough to the bar that even the town's shadiest life forms would be willing to partake.

Anyhow, this one year, the clowns were doing their stuff – getting shit-hammered at the bar and heckling tourists. The rodeo clowns were in fine form, too, cracking up the crowd with their

BETTER YET, HE HAD A FAKE ARSE – A DEAD-SET PLASTIC BUM.

half-time show. To us kids, it was classic. One clown dropped his dacks and mooned the crowd. That's straight out of How to Entertain a Teenage Boy 101. Better yet, he had a fake arse – a dead-set plastic bum. So just when the more excitable in the crowd had realised he'd in fact been having us on, he dropped the plastic one and let the crowd have it with the Real McCoy. And what a sight. He'd tattooed a 'W' on each cheek and named his arse the 'WoW factor'. Genius stuff. Women shrieked. Children screamed. Dad laughed and I scheduled an appointment in my head to get the very same tattoo done the day I realised my dream of playing for the Wallabies. And I never break a promise or back out of a deal… No pun intended.

BOATING BALLS-UP

If you've ever been deep-water fishing and had to launch your dinghy from the shore, then I'm certain you can sympathise with this next yarn. If you can't, you're a rotten bastard and a liar.

The old man wasn't renowned for his patience. Yeah, I'll be darned, a schoolteacher with a quick temper... Anyhow, he sure as shit wasn't gonna wait for some bludger tourists at the boat ramp to back their trailers in all day so he came up with another play – beach launch. Now, for the uninitiated, a beach launch is difficult enough with two blokes, let alone a family of 10.

It basically requires pushing the boat through the waves and everyone trying to climb in without tipping the boat or before a wave smashes over ya head – the fishing equivalent of patting your head and rubbing your stomach.

Us kids used to hold the boat for the old man while he'd battle the waves to jump in, start her up and give the signal for us to join him. At the appropriate time, Dad would call 'all in' and we'd proceed to scramble, claw, pull and punch to make it aboard. The old boy would get sea sick at our attempt just to enter, at which point he'd call 'all out'. It was basically a to and fro of 'all in' and 'all out' until one of us would near dislocate a hip in an attempt to synchronise our entrance. It required us all channelling our inner Go Go Gadget and Rubber Man.

As usual, the crowd gathered on the beach to see the poor man's Brady Bunch risk life and death all in the name of a few flathead. Worse yet, most were so embarrassed on our behalf that they never even submitted the footage to *Funniest Home Videos*.

But on this particular day, we averted disaster and made it safely out to sea. I dominated with the hook and sinker and from what I'm about to tell I think it's safe to surmise that the old man dominated the esky – and XXXX Bitter inside. That's Bitter *not* Gold. As Dad always said, 'You don't make friends with Gold'. It's here I'd like to take a quick timeout to suggest you always drink responsibly and in moderation. Because you make fewer friends as a drunk arsehole.

FROM WHAT I'M ABOUT TO TELL I THINK IT'S SAFE TO SURMISE THAT THE OLD MAN DOMINATED THE ESKY

Anyhow, after a successful day at sea we returned to where the waves were breaking for what we expected to be a relatively easy landing by comparison to our entrance. As we moved towards shore, we all braced for action. We'd come in behind a wave and Dad would jump out, steady the ship and take us safely to shore. Well, this is where that Bitter comes in. Because the bloke was seriously disoriented he jumped directly into a deep hole and disappeared from view with only his tracksuit top and terry towelling hat floating to the surface.

We didn't know whether to laugh or cry but, to be quite honest, we didn't have either option, because another wave was about to crash on us and we were a rudderless ship without our captain heading directly for shore.

Luckily, the beach was now full of Japanese tourists – who are never short of a good chat or a camera – and were clicking away with their cameras. We felt like mongs, Dad looked like a clown and the puzzled Japanese tourists were confused to say the least at what they determined to be standard Australian boating practice. It was a humbling experience. And only fitting that the tourists got the last laugh. I've been sympathetic of tourists and a respectful traveller ever since.

"MATE UH, THE LOCKS, YOU UH YOU UH EVER HEARD OF THAT BIBLE STORY OF UM SAMSON AND DELILAH? – ('YEAH YEAH YEAH NO') – WELL, IT'S GOT NOTHING TO DO WITH WHAT I'M DOING, SO..."

TRANSLATION: 'I'd prefer to be left alone right now.'

HIGH SEAS BATTLE

We'd just bought the new family boat – a quick one – and it was time for its first mission. Like any fisherman will tell you, it's imperative to get up before dawn and beat the wind. But more importantly, beat the other bastards who wanna lay claim to the good fishing spots before you do.

So sure enough, the old man had us up before we'd barely gotten some shut-eye. I could have sworn the 11 pm News was on. And did I mention it was a school night?

Anyhow, there were more important things at hand – like testing out the new boat. We hit the Gold Coast Broadwater at dark, erased any trace of our being there – which isn't as shady as it seems – and disappeared into the night. Okay, that did sound pretty dodgy. And if you count my sleeping brother in the hull, then we were carrying a body, too. And the current was running… Time-out! This is getting creepy, even for me.

So, after a delightful cruise we anchored just off Wave Break Island and looked for a good place to drop the body. Sorry, anchor…

We pulled up next to a red buoy and began preparing for action. Worms? Check. Prawns? Check. White bait? Check. Lures? Check? Squidgies? Just what the F*&k are these new things?

Anyways, you get the picture. And quite frankly, it was all for nothing. Because an hour later, and the sun even now barely up, we'd caught nothing. Zero. Zip. We'd come up like a bloke after his divorce hearing – empty-handed.

Making matters worse, this other bastard about 20 metres up the shore was pulling in so many fish he may as well have been a trawler. It was demoralising. And it was hard as hell to get my homework done while Dad was cursing him. It was almost like the other bloke was taunting us. And you'd think that too if you saw him move his lamp to shine a blazing light on his haul. He wouldn't give us a clue either. The kind of bloke who if he owned the ocean wouldn't give you a wave. And you sure as shit wouldn't get your hands on his first Rolo, let alone his last.

By now, patient old Dad had had enough. And decided to cast where old mate was. Even in the dark his aim was spot on, Dad's sinker clocked old mate's lamp dead on, smashing the light to smithereens. To suggest the other fisherman was unhappy is an understatement of Benn Robinson proportions.

THAT'S BIG BROTHER NATHAN DOING HIS BEST TO KEEP ME UPRIGHT. I'M TOLD I WEIGHED THE SAME AT FOUR MONTHS AS NATHAN DID AGED FOUR YEARS.

MY THIRD BIRTHDAY PARTY. DAD WAS IN CHARGE OF FIRE SAFETY BUT LUCKILY NOT THE CAKE - THAT WAS MUM'S AREA. CAN'T BEAT MUM'S SPONGE CAKE. LIKE DARRYL KERRIGAN SAYS, 'IT'S WHAT YA DO WITH IT.'

ALWAYS IN THE YARD, KICKING WHATEVER WAS AROUND. MANY A DOLL WAS TORPEDOED OVER THE FENCE TO MY SISTER'S HORROR. 'DON'T WORRY, THEIR DOG WILL TAKE CARE OF IT...'

LUKE SIGNALLING HIS PLEASURE AT BEING PART OF THE PHOTO. FROM LEFT TO RIGHT: LUKE, ME, LIZZY AND JAKE.

WITH THE OLD BOY AT THE PRESENTATION OF MY QUEENSLAND SCHOOLBOY'S JERSEY. I WAS 16 AND KNEW EVERYTHING.

A YOUNG BADGE, FRESHLY 18, AFTER AUSTRALIA EXITED THE HONG KONG 2007 IRB SEVENS WORLD SERIES. GRINNING LIKE A CHESHIRE CAT AFTER RELUCTANTLY SIGNING AN ENGLISH WOMAN'S CHEST.

MY FIRST HAT-TRICK FOR THE FORCE. WITH TWO TURNIN' AND TWO BURNIN' I TOOK AN INTERCEPT AND WENT LENGTH. THERE WERE REPORTS OF BLACK SMOKE SEEN BY THE SPECTATORS AT THE 50 METRE MARK. THREE IN A ROW AGAINST THE WARATAHS.

THE AUSTRALIAN COMMONWEALTH GAMES SWIMMING TEAM GETTING ON THE BURST AFTER A SOLID DAY OF RACES, DELHI 2010. MANY A BAD DECISION WAS MADE AT THE AFTER PARTY...

REHYDRATING WITH BEN TAPUAI AFTER A VICTORY AGAINST ENGLAND, NOVEMBER 2012.

BAGGING SOME MEAT FOR THE BARBARIANS VS THE WALLABIES AT TWICKENHAM, NOVEMBER 2014. ONE OF THE MORE PROFESSIONAL OUTFITS I'VE BEEN A PART OF.

LIFE ON TOUR INVOLVES A LOT OF THIS SORT OF BUSINESS: HOTELS, COACHES, AIRPORTS. THIS IS ME AND TETERA FAULKNER TRYING NOT TO MISS OUR NEXT FLIGHT SOMEWHERE IN SOUTH AMERICA.

THIS PHOTO WAS SNAPPED AHEAD OF A WESTERN FORCE AND SOUTHERN KINGS GAME IN SOUTH AFRICA. TOWARD THE END OF THE SESSION WE CHASED OFF A BLOKE HIDING IN THE BUSHES FILMING OUR EVERY MOVE. FUNNILY ENOUGH, ON MATCH DAY THE KINGS SEEMED TO KNOW ALL OUR TACTICS AND TOOK US TO THE CLEANERS.

JUNE 2014. CELEBRATING A BIG WIN OVER THE FROGS. THAT'S MY COMMERCIAL MANAGER JOSH WHITE IN THE GREEN JACKET. MY BROTHER JAKE IS LOOKING OVER MY SHOULDER.

BACKSTAGE WITH OLD MATE ABOUT TO SHOOT A TV COMMERCIAL FOR A BIG SHAMPOO BRAND - MY FIRST MAJOR ENDORSEMENT CAMPAIGN.

I RENTED THIS BEAST IN SIEM REAP, CAMBODIA DURING THE WET SEASON. I TOOK THESE KIDS FOR A BURN AND WE ALL CAME BACK COVERED IN MUD.

DURING MY SOLO TOUR OF CAMBODIA, ENJOYING A BIT OF 'ME TIME.' WATERFALL, UKULELE AND A BEER. JUST NEED A SHEILA...

STANDARD KIT FOR FIRING ROCKET PROPELLED GRENADES IN THE WILDS OF CAMBODIA. A YOUNG MAN TRYING TO FIND HIMSELF...

IN THE MOUNTAINS OF NORWAY AT THE WINTER HOUSE OF THIS VIKING WOMAN. WEARING TRADITIONAL *BUNAD* (NATIONAL COSTUME), BLONDE HAIR AND BLUE EYES...

WHEN SHE BAILS YOU UP ON A CLIFF FACE AND PUTS THE HARD WORD ON YA... CLIFF JUMPING IN INDONESIA.

AT A GAME PARK IN SOUTH AFRICA, WHEN THINGS TURNED AGGRESSIVE AFTER PLAY WRESTLING. STILL GOT THE SCAR - THEY'RE BLOODY STRONG FOR THEIR SIZE!

TIMON THE MEERKAT WATCHING MY BACK... FUNNY LITTLE BUGGERS. GAME PARK, SOUTH AFRICA.

PATTING A TIGER IN JO'BERG. THIS CAT LET ME PUT MY HAND IN HER MOUTH AND DID ME THE COURTESY OF NOT BITING IT OFF.

DOUBLE ISLAND POINT, QUEENSLAND. NOT A BAD SPOT FOR A WAVE ON ME OLD MAN'S KINGSLEY. A GREAT FAMILY DESTINATION AND MANY MEMORIES. CAN HANG LOOSE.

FISHING WITH ME OLD MATE BLAIR (BIGGEST CAGS ON THE EAST COAST). *EL CAPITÁN* ENJOYING LEADING THE FISH COUNT AGAIN. HE COMPLAINS, 'MY ROD'S TOO SMALL.' CORRECT!

KALBARRI, WA. A SWAG, WHEELS, UKULELE AND THE QUICK BOAT STRAPPED TO THE ROOF. POSSIBLY A FEW TINS...

MONGOLIA, 2014. WE HAD A GOOD HUNT. YOU SHOULD SEE THE MITTS ON A GOLDEN EAGLE - IMPRESSIVE! THE NOMADS AREN'T SHY ON THE VODKA EITHER... STREWTH!

THIS PHOTO WAS TAKEN AT THE RED SPARKS' SUMMER TRAINING CAMP JUST HOURS AFTER I ARRIVED IN JAPAN FOR THE FIRST TIME. I'M NOT SURE WHAT WAS MORE DIFFICULT - ATTEMPTING TO INTRODUCE MYSELF TO MY NEW TEAM-MATES OR USING CHOPSTICKS FOR THE FIRST TIME.

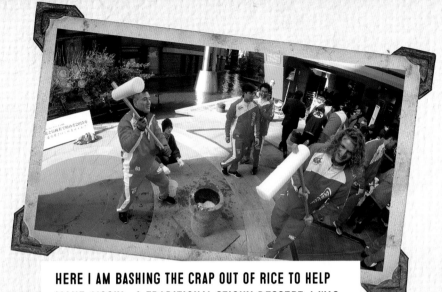

HERE I AM BASHING THE CRAP OUT OF RICE TO HELP MAKE *MOCHI* - A TRADITIONAL STICKY DESSERT. I WAS A BIT CLUMSY AND ENDED UP BUSTING A CHUNK OUT OF THE STONE MORTAR.

THIS IS MY LOCAL BAIT SHOP IN FUKUOKA. THE OLD DUCK ALWAYS HAS A SMILE ON HER DIAL. I'VE SNAGGED MYSELF A FREE BAG OF WORMS IN THIS SHOT.

HOW COULD YOU LOSE WITH A CHEER SQUAD LIKE THIS? UNFORTUNATELY WE DID (AGAINST SOUTH AFRICA IN BRISBANE, 2013)!

MENDOZA, ARGENTINA, JULY 2015.
CELEBRATING A WIN WITH THE WALLABY SQUAD.

The bloke must have been a taxidermist because he suggested some pretty intricate forms of retribution before cutting the old man's line and giving a solid 'up yours' to a boat full of schoolkids.

With the wisdom of Solomon and the fortitude of his infant daughter, Dad said 'Let's go!' and ripped at the anchor like his life depended on it. Which all things considered, it kind of did. But there was a problem. Remember that red buoy we'd anchored next to? Well, yeah, the anchor had become twisted around it. Shit!

We circled the bloody thing like we were racing it for a good 10 minutes before the now highly anxious old man gave the order – 'Cut the bastard!' And we sawed off our brand new anchor on our brand new boat and burned off into the rising sun leaving many a fish, our anchor and our dignity. Average day.

"WHEN THE START OF THE SEASON TURNS UP, THE BOYS WILL BE UH, GOIN' OFF LIKE A BULL IN A CHINA SHOP."

TRANSLATION: 'Bulls are big, aggressive animals that don't take kindly to being to being held in tight spaces. China is a delicate form of porcelain that's easily broken. The two don't mix well together and were a bull to be led into a china shop, one can only assume he'd kick anything and everything to get out. A show of strength and power.'

BUCCANEER SPIRIT

When I was up in Bundy I remember a game I played with the Buccaneers. Safe to say we won it because I only have enough gigabytes to store the winning games.

Anyhow, it was classic country footy. The field had line markings that were barely visible, like they'd let the local pre-schoolers at it with some hand-me-down chalk and it was situated between a cow paddock and a small crop plantation. And in all honesty, that was one of the best pitches we played on. Though it was that rough it was akin to running the 100 metres on loose gravel in bare feet.

But I digress. I'd found myself coming off the bench – a travesty given me own bloody brother Luke was captain – and I was playing out wide next to a short stocky bloke who looked like a cannonball with fingers and toes. If I wasn't already feeling hard

I WAS PLAYING OUT WIDE NEXT TO A SHORT STOCKY BLOKE WHO LOOKED LIKE A CANNONBALL WITH FINGERS AND TOES.

done by having to come off the bench, it was no shot in the arm when I noticed the nugget seemed to have wobbly legs and was struggling to stand let alone chat. I'm inquisitive at the best of times and was determined to get this bloke's story – who was he, where was he from and what the hell did his training and nutrition program consist of?

So during the game I was talking to him, calling the plays and getting ready to launch an attack. But still, something didn't seem quite right…

It was only a matter of time before I went on the burst and sure enough a few minutes later Luke – playing flyhalf – gave me a good seed and the Buccaneers were on the attack!

I put the foot down, threw in a goosestep to shake things up and turned on the gas to go flying through a gap in the defence. I dodged a few potholes in the pitch, the odd cow and stick of corn, then drew the last few remaining defenders in as I looked to offload to the massive Minion – but he was nowhere to be seen! And after we'd built such a rapport…

After the game the beers were flowing, as they often did, and the team was belting out the team song – which I'm pretty sure was just the Hard Yakka jingle. I let my new-found mate enjoy a few sips before I asked him the pivotal question – 'Where were you out there?'

He lifted his his head and squinted his eyes: 'I had a full bottle of rum in me. The mind was willing but the jelly sticks couldn't keep up!'

And he was the player–coach! Jokes. Good bloke but.

"ONE OF ME OLD MAN'S SAYINGS, THAT IF YOU WANNA MAKE GOD LAUGH, YOU TELL HIM YOUR PLANS. "

TRANSLATION: 'The best laid plans often go awry. So live in the moment. Take it as it comes and lower your expectations. You're less likely to be disappointed and more likely to enjoy yourself.'

LONGREACH, FAR-OUT!

Before I was bashing down the door as a Wallaby great or even realised my undeniable ability – ha! – even I'm struggling to keep a straight face – I joined a rugby tour that was headed out to the 'Stockman's Capital of Australia' – Longreach.

If you haven't heard of the joint it's in outback Queensland, is the birthplace of Qantas and can be can summed up in two words – F---ing hot!

Anywho, during the team briefing the coach said there was to be no alcohol for anyone until the trip home. First thing on my mind: 'Who does this bloke think he is? Me missus? And where'd he think we were headed? The in-laws?'

Protests aside, we got on the bus with high hopes and a professional attitude for that 12-hour demoralising haul to

Longreach, traversing through country more scene-less than downtown Kingsford.

It didn't take long before a few of us got to playing poker on an esky lid with loose change.

Moe was the money man and he always had a bumbag full of coins – God only knows where he got that fashion atrocity from. If the bumbag were an animal, its species would have been culled into extinction years ago.

But Moe's fashion nonsense aside, he was the man with the coins. And if you gave him 20 bucks you'd be lucky to get $10 in change – and they say casino odds are steep! His conversion rate was worse than the big banks so my brothers always had a few playing cards tucked into their pockets to counter any losses from the buy-in. Genius.

Needless to say, any latecomers were subject to Moe's weakening exchange rate, Luke and Nath's card racket and an ever-present flatulence problem – is this becoming a running theme?

It was a good way to burn a few hours but in a beat-up bus in outback Queensland, with 30 sweaty blokes and nine odd hours still to go, the professional manner of our motley crew was quickly fading. And the bus driver didn't take kindly.

Finally, the bus came to an abrupt stop and the bus driver marched down the back and in no uncertain terms made clear his disdain for whoever was smoking. There aren't enough dashes to fill in that sentence…

And no sooner had he asked 'who was smoking' than the dunny door flew open to reveal a dishevelled figure in a haze of smoke, complete with bloodshot eyes. He looked the driver dead in the eye and said 'Smoking? Not me.' That was all the encouragement the boys needed to trade in the professionalism for some good old-fashioned footy trip antics.

As soon as the bus stopped for fuel, cartons of beer began being loaded onto the bus like sandbags during a flood. The only thing professional about this outfit was the precision with which the boys worked in unison to form a human chain and pass the cartons along. Not a single casualty either, thank you.

The bus trip ended up being red-hot and the boys pulled it together on the field, too. Remarkably, the tour was a success!

But one thing those fancy Longreach brochures don't warn you about is the flies! I hadn't seen so many since I left my bedroom! They were that bad you had to eat your meat pie under your shirt to stop the flies from getting in ya mouth…

"**THE FLAMBOYANT FRENCH? THEY LOOK ALL RIGHT. THEY HAVE A GOOD STYLE ABOUT THEM WITH THEIR HAIRDOS. I MIGHT TAKE A FEW POINTERS AND GO TO A STYLIST TO SORT MYSELF OUT. A FEW OF THE BOYS TELL ME I LOOK A BIT ORDINARY AT TIMES.**"

TRANSLATION: 'I agree that French people are traditionally considered stylish and, if given the opportunity, I'd be more than happy to consider changing up my look to be more fashion forward.'

BUSH BASHING

I played in Bargara once. Which shouldn't come as too much of a surprise given it's about a 10-minute drive from the main drag of Bundaberg.

Anyways, it's a nice little joint near Mon Repos (swear I didn't make that name up), a well-known green zone and turtle rookery on the Queensland coast.

It always stood out as a unique place 'cause the rugby posts were bent over almost 90 degrees due to a cyclone that smashed the place some time back.

Even by country rugby standards, it was a rough park. It had a grass athletic track around the field, a heavy slope that saw you running uphill half the game and more faecal matter than a dog track. And personally, I loved it. Such things give a place character.

Or it could have been because the joint backed onto a nudist beach which gave it that little spark that it needed. Let's just say six of one, a full dozen of the other...

THIS BLOKE HAD SO MUCH PULL I EVEN REMEMBER HIM HAVING THE PUB RE-OPENED ONE NIGHT WITH NOTHING MORE THAN THE WINK OF AN EYE.

I remember being in the car after the game and someone asking the locally renowned coach, Rob Darney: 'You ever broken the law, Coach?' Like Tony Abbott in relation to misogynist allegations, Coach responded without hesitation: 'I am the Law!'

This bloke had so much pull I even remember him having the pub re-opened one night with nothing more than the wink of an eye.

He was like a real-life Chuck Norris. Or Tony Soprano? He instilled fear in any obstacle he tackled.

I remember on a boys' trip to Rainbow Beach and Fraser Island the sandy four-wheel-drive track was impassable. LandCruisers and Troopies were backed up for miles while a bulldozer attempted to fix the gaping hole in the track. But Coach wasn't having any of that.

Like the King of Westeros, he commanded everyone – including the dozer operator – to get the BLEEP out of the way, 'cause he was coming through. We were in the backseat and didn't know whether to cry or cheer. We settled on both.

Next thing we know Coach's foot was flat to the floor, the engine was screaming and sand was spraying onlookers like bullets. The wheels were spinning in full fury. We hit the incline flat-out and the vehicle, passengers, esky and all were airborne.

We got ourselves in the brace position but Coach, calm as you like, window down and his arm resting on the door trim, turned his head to a group of astounded backpackers as he powered through thin air and yelled 'We're Aussies!'

He cleared the hole with ease. A perfect 10. And didn't spill a drop of what I can only presume was Bundaberg Ginger Beer. It's hard to tell in a brown paper bag.

Rob Darney was legit. So when he swore to me he could run the 100 metres in 10.7 seconds, it was just easier to believe him.

"MY OLD MAN WOKE ME UP IN THE MORNING. HE WAS GOING OFF LIKE A BAG OF CATS. "

TRANSLATION: 'Cats are loners that typically like to roam free. They don't take kindly to being put in close quarters with other cats and get quite physical.'

DUCK!

The year 2001. We'd survived Y2K without a scratch on us and I was well on my way to manhood and all the glory it holds. I was in Year 9. Fourteen years of age. I had the world at my feet. And my two younger brothers, Jake and Joe, at my beck and call. I mightn't have been the biggest bloke but I was a giant in comparison to those little grubs. Who I love dearly, of course.

Anyhow, Dad had told us not to muck around with any of his equipment in the shed. Which of course in teenager speak translates to: 'Go on, lads. Do your worst. I'd be filthy if you didn't.'

It was like waving a Redskin in front of a schoolkid. So we took on off up there with grand plans to make a bow and arrow from PVC pipe – I'd seen *MacGyver* once or twice and if Bear Grylls asks, I was ahead of my time.

I MIGHTN'T HAVE BEEN THE BIGGEST BLOKE BUT I WAS A GIANT IN COMPARISON TO THOSE LITTLE GRUBS.

But all of a sudden I hear a chirping sound. Instantly, I thought one of the chooks had got out of the cage. Not 'cage' cage. The bludgers were free to roam. Free-range organic even by suburban standards. But to my surprise it was a family of ducks. Six ducklings, in fact, that were running along the yard. Then I spotted mother duck (not slanging here) about 20 yards in front of the pack. Yes! The coast was clear. So I swooped down and picked up a duckling to get a closer look. The duckling then made a certain sound different to the other ducks. It was tough to describe the sound – a combination of standing on a dog's tail and Dad's night snorts.

Smelling a rat, I looked up to see the mother duck taking off and coming right for me. I was used to sheilas making a quick dash in my direction at the school dance but what this duck was offering I wanted no part of. Not to say I didn't wanna see what happened…

So I quickly palmed the duckling off to Jake, who was all of eight years old, stepped back and thought to myself: 'Nick, you genius. You've done it again'. Jake looked more confused than Tony Abbott at the Oxford Street Markets. Jake looked up at me and saw a guilty grin on my face and then his face went white – he turned to hear a horrible hissing sound – like something breaking the sound barrier – and did so just in time for the mother duck to hit him in the jugular at 186,000 miles per second or, some would say, the speed of light.

The impact was brutal. Jake fell backward, the duckling catapulted into the air and landed on the shed roof.

It gave new meaning to the term 'duck' both literally and figuratively. And that look of sheer fear on Jake's face was priceless.

We near copped a hiding from the old man that night. Not because we went into his shed but because 'none of you morons had the foresight to take the video camera with you?'

To this day his one goal in life remains to get on *Funniest Home Videos*.

"I JUST SAW THE LINE, PINNED ME EARS BACK AND ENDED BAGGING A BIT OF MEAT IN THE CORNER THERE, WHICH WAS TOPS!"

TRANSLATION: 'Meat pie is rhyming slang for try. I don't care for the extra syllable and it's my birthright as an Australian to minimise even slang terms. Therefore, meat is short for meat pie which is slang for try. And I love me some meat.'

ANYTHING FOR A BUCK

I've never been one for hard labour. Hell, that's why I became a winger and not a forward.

So it'll come as little surprise to you that I'd conjure up any scheme possible to make money and avoid hard work as a youngster.

I was some 13 years of age. Finally, a teenager. And in *Game of Thrones* years, old enough to conquer a people and pillage the village. I knew what I wanted to pillage – the local lolly shop for Killer Pythons and race cars. But how would I conquer the people and convince them to give me their hard-earned? A light bulb moment – food challenge!

Even now looking back, offering to eat a carton of raw eggs for the enjoyment of strangers was a stroke of genius.

We were in Bargara, a coastal town near Bundaberg, and my holiday funds had dried up. Asking for pocket money from the old man was a sure way to get laughed at or told to bugger off. So one day when we were having a BBQ in the park by the beach I saw an opportunity. There were people everywhere and though they wouldn't say it, they were begging to be entertained. Enter one N. Cummins.

I foraged through the esky and found a carton of eggs and of the few things I knew to be true in this world, it was that no one likes raw eggs. Let alone watching someone consume them.

'No, we won't be using them today', were Mum's words. Basically a seal of approval.

So I marched out into the middle of the park and commanded the attention of my soon-to-be audience: 'How much for me to eat this carton of raw eggs?'

I was doing the carnies down at Darling Harbour proud. I spun the spotlight on the audience and sure enough, they started to cough up some cash. I'm not certain whether they were excited or just desperate for me to leave them alone, but the gold coins starting coming in and then some notes started appearing. Shit, life as a travelling freak show wasn't seeming so bad.

So with anticipation building – State of Origin-esque you might say – this magician was in need of a beautiful assistant. Preferably blonde, buxom and some years younger than me. But seeing as though I was 13 and on a family vacation – in Bargara – I had little choice but to employ the services of my four-year-old brother as my assistant. He's turned into a sort, too – if you're into that type of thing, ladies.

Anyhow, the show must go on. And he held the carton up as I began cracking the eggs on my front teeth, one by one, and swallowing them whole.

I wasn't sure how my guts were gonna take it but I'd had Dad's green curry plenty and lived to tell the tale so I was confident these hyena guts would pull through. And sure enough they did, and I bagged $40 in less than 10 minutes. I've never been able to match that rate since.

However, upon leaving the park and heading home in the family vehicle, the guts began to take a turn for the worse. It sounded like a wild boar watching a horror movie. And with 200 metres till home, I couldn't hold much longer and dropped an ungodly aroma. The screams were instant from my sisters and I couldn't deny it – blame it on the unleaded gas vapours. Everybody knew what I'd eaten – a dozen of Woolies finest.

The car came to an immediate halt and I was evicted with force – not for the first or last time.

Walking home, all I could think was 'suckers!' They were trapped in it and I was out free, the wind at my nose. And my tail…

IT SOUNDED LIKE A WILD BOAR WATCHING A HORROR MOVIE.

"IF I GET A GIG, I'M GONNA GO OFF LIKE A CUT SNAKE."

TRANSLATION: 'Snakes don't have legs. They slither smoothly. However, when cut by machete or shovel they tend to become angry and their movements very aggressive.'

GUINEA PIG ISLAND

The family had just moved to Chambers Flat and there was a lot to explore for a young buck like me – especially down at the dam that had been recently dug out. Were there prehistoric bones? Treasure? Or buried cars?

After a solid storm, the dam was about half full and the island in the middle (about 5 by 5 metres) was now not accessible – by foot that is. So one day I was working up in the chook pen and thought 'maybe we whack a few of these squawkers on the island to spice things up a bit. Their very own motte, if you will.'

So I made sure their wings were clipped and took them down to the dam. Doing my best impersonation of Trevor Hendy, I paddled across with one hand on one of Dad's old surf skis while still holding the bird. I released the chook and dusted off my shoulders: 'Nick, you genius'.

But within about 20 minutes of deploying said bird it had jumped into the water and swum across to the mainland. Was I witnessing magic? A Guinness World Record-breaking chicken? Who knew the bastards could swim?

So before I got Dad's camera out and gave the Ripley's Believe It Or Not lads a ring, I took another chicken out there. Same thing. This happened two more times, after which I decided they'd won their freedom.

Disappointed, my dreams of fame dashed and realising I had regular, non-magic chickens, I put the chooks back. But not before bleakness turned into a glory and I spotted my sister's guinea pig.

Without asking – sibling code – I quickly snuck off with the pig and paddled across. Set a new lap record in fact. The little tacker carefully walked up to the hollow of the island's solitary tree and we didn't see him until the next day. He would become the first settler on Pig Island. Some say the show *Survivor* was conceived that very day. On that very island. By some, I mean me. And I'm still waiting on those royalty cheques, Jeff Probst.

Anyhow, the only way to feed him was a lettuce via grenade throw. On impact, the pig would tear a hamstring to get out there and start

THE ONLY WAY TO FEED HIM WAS A LETTUCE VIA GRENADE THROW.

gorging. It was faultless. Until one day when he was on the chew something spooked him. He was minding his own business when a hawk came tearing down and near snatched him, just missing him. During the pig's impressive acceleration back to the hollow it let out the type of squeal I've become quite used to in years since – it sounded like a high-pitched 'ewwwww'. And every time I get knocked back by a bird at the bar it reminds me of that little bastard.

Anyhow, it got to the point where a leaf would fall out of the tree and the pig would squeal and hammer off. I like to tell myself he found Mohammed and decided to fast. But truth be told, he died on that island. And it's how my sister would have wanted it...

"HE'S A PRETTY QUICK ROOSTER ALRIGHT. YOUDON'T SHOW HIM THESIDELINE THAT'S FORSURE. "

TRANSLATION: 'The rooster is the king of the hen house and if he gets a sniff of an opportunity to make a break, he'll take it and often make something of it. Therefore, you need to keep an eye on him.'

FEATHERED TERRORIST

Back on the acreage about 2001 and I'd recently been christened a teenager with the big 13th birthday. And with the honour comes a certain sense of responsibility. You can't just be scared of things any more. You gotta take matters into your own hands and confront life's woes head-on or your mates and older brothers will make fun of you. Now, if avoiding ridicule, humiliation and peer pressure isn't justification enough to act on impulse, then what is? Around this time I'd become mates with a kid from school name of Tom Magee – still mates with him today in fact.

We'd ride our bikes everywhere together, happy as can be, until the one season every schoolkid dreads – spring. Otherwise known as magpie swooping season.

On a daily basis riding between one another's houses we would be violently attacked by one black and white devil in particular. I'm not sure what his problem was exactly but he took particular exception to Tom and myself. And it got to a point where out of fear, Tom flat-out refused to make the ride. Selfish prick. That meant if I wanted to hang out with my mate, I'd have to brave the gauntlet and put my noggin on the line to make it to the Magee residence.

Parents, listen up: If you want your kids to wear helmets but can't convince them, have a couple of magpies relocated to the neighbourhood and they'll be begging for new Stackhats.

Anyhow, I dusted off the melon protector, kissed the loved ones goodbye and headed off on the daunting journey. This was Tom Cruise *Mission: Impossible* stuff and TC, if you're reading, you might consider the inclusion of paternal magpies in your next plot.

So it was, I made my approach to the danger zone and spotted the little bastard waiting up on the power line. I don't even think he had any birdlings, just a grudge against the world and a penchant for pain.

With my heart pounding I accelerated to full speed. And the magpie didn't move as I passed by at full tilt. But classic magpie, he waited until my back was turned to launch his attack. Bloody king hits are a coward's move. And just when I thought I was in the clear I heard that death knell squawk and knew I had him right on my six o'clock.

I had no means to retaliate so resorted to the tried and true tactic every Australian has employed at one time or another and frantically began to wave my hand in the air to scare it off.

I counted to three and threw my hand up in the air just before impact and somehow got hold of the thing! Now I've got him pecking furiously at my hand and I'm more scared than ever. I flick it off and somehow, someway, he loses his draught and goes straight under my back wheel! 'Shit! Now I'm a murderer.' I turned back, expecting the worst, only to see the crafty bastard dusting himself off then disappearing into the sky like a fart in a fan factory.

I'm not proud of my actions. But I can proudly say no birds were harmed in this story.

As for Magee, you can only imagine what his nickname was for the rest of that school year...

"WHEN YOU COME INTO THIS SORT OF GAME YOU'VE GOT TO SHOW THE PATIENCE OF THE DALAI LAMA INITIALLY IN ORDER TO GET THAT GIG AND WHEN IT COMES ROUND BE READY TO STRIKE. "

TRANSLATION: 'In order to be successful one must possess both patience and ability to attack with force when necessary. Kind of like a Dalai Ninja. Now, that's an idea!'

BADGER ON SAFARI

Before rugby tours of South Africa were part of my life, I'd made a trip over there back in 2009 for a safari and to experience nature in its most raw form.

At this particular safari park we are escorted around by a European backpacker on work experience, who showed us through various enclosures housing large cats.

The tigers were about one metre tall and to my surprise were only just cubs – they were still being weaned off the bottle. 'Harmless' I thought to myself. So after seeing one of the expert trainers put her hand in the tiger's mouth, I took the opportunity to do the same as soon as she wasn't looking.

And to my surprise, it just started sucking on my fingers. But the boys weren't to know that and when they turned around to see my hand deep in the jaws of one of nature's deadliest killing machines, they were shocked!

I was a bit of a legend and didn't hate the attention. So later on in the lion cage and with my confidence sky high, I had no qualms

I HAD NO QUALMS WRESTLING A LION CUB THE SIZE OF A MEDIUM DOG

wrestling a lion cub the size of a medium dog – only for the mongrel to bite me on the bicep and draw blood. 'Wallaby survives Lions!' the headline would have read had anyone known I'd grow up to be the Wallabies' fifth-best winger in 2015.

Driving through the same game reserve we were delayed by two big male elephants bluing on the dirt track – reminded me of a few of the props at 3 am trying to impress the last woman standing. Bloody forwards…

Unlike said woman, we attempted to move closer. The plan was to kind of scare them out of the way. But with the elephants being one and a half times the size of the van we were driving they were hardly intimidated by our Tarago. In fact, all our presence did was piss them off enough for one to charge the van. You should have heard the high-pitch screams of panic coming from a group of burly rugby players – and Nathan Charles wasn't even there!

Our guard slammed it in reverse and floored it. Then the big unit stopped, stood tall and sounded his big trumpet as if to claim victory.

Upon reflection, there may have been a small amount in the undies. Awesome animal.

Upon further reflection, perhaps I should steer clear of live animals altogether. I mean, how many different species can I be attacked by?

"SWEATIN' LIKE A GYPSY WITH A MORTGAGE. "

TRANSLATION: 'Gypsies, while good people for the most part, are largely low-income earners. Their work often involves travelling from town to town with a travelling carnival or fair. Weather often plays a significant factor in their earning ability. Therefore, should a Gypsy put away enough to secure a loan on a permanent residence, their ability to pay it off is at the mercy of the weather and the small towns they pass through. It can result in sleepless nights and perspiration.'

SONNY BILL'S GOLDEN SHOULDER

It was 2010 on a training day in sunny Perth. And the boys and I were undergoing a compulsory test that measures your reaction time and cognitive function. Basically, this test serves as base level data so if down the track you become concussed in a match – or at training, God forbid – the doctors can carry out the same test and compare it to the original data – and see by percentages how much dumber you've become. It's just another way the government has to control your mind. I'm certain there was some sort of chip implanted.

Jokes aside, just a few weeks later we were up against the Chiefs and I must have been causing them all sorts of headaches because before I knew it, I'd copped a shoulder to the melon at a ruck 15 minutes in and went down like a sack of spuds. I was out

I WAS OUT FOR A COUPLE OF SECONDS BUT WHEN I CAME TO I FELT GOOD AS XXXX GOLD

for a couple of seconds but when I came to I felt good as XXXX Gold and got stuck right back in.

Anyhow, after the game I was shaking hands with Sonny Bill Williams – and just quietly there is some truth to the rumour he left rugby because I was intimidating him. And Sonny says to me: 'You nearly got me there!' I laughed, cocked my head and thought 'What the hell is he talking about?'

I didn't and don't remember the game at all. But had a ripper of a match, I'm told.

And it's kinda weird when you watch footage of the game and see what you did.

Well, come Monday and the team doctor asked me to do the cognitive function test and upon conclusion he was very concerned. 'The scores are very different,' he says, shaking his head. 'Shit! My career's over' was my first thought. Quickly

'SHIT! MY CAREER'S OVER' WAS MY FIRST THOUGHT.

followed by a quick SMS to the blokes at NASA to let them know I wouldn't be able to accept the rocket scientist position.

'How different?' I asked. The doc took his time. Adjusted his glasses and then looked earnestly into my eyes… We shared a little moment and then he says: 'Your reaction time and cognitive functions are 33 per cent faster and your scores are on average 30 per cent better'. And all because that big bastard Sonny Bill knocked some sense into me! And if they were the results, maybe I wasn't hit around the head enough as a baby?

I've been running head-first at Sonny Bill at every opportunity since. Told ya he left rugby because of me... But he obviously missed me enough to come back again.

"YOU GAVE A LOT OF PILL TO THE BADGE ... WHICH WAS GOOD OF YOU. "

TRANSLATION: 'Get used to me talking of myself in the third person from here on out.'

A FORCE TO BE RECKONED WITH PART: 2

In 2011 the Western Force decided on a two-week tour to Samoa to play two games against the national side. 'You beauty, holiday!' I thought to myself.

But it was anything but. They were some of the most brutal games I've ever been involved

THEY WERE SOME OF THE MOST BRUTAL GAMES I'VE EVER BEEN INVOLVED WITH.

with. You know Samoans – they're the big, strong, fast players on almost every footy field. Hell, even Dwayne 'The Rock' Johnson is Samoan.

And on this trip, The Rock himself must have been in the crowd because the local lads were out to impress. They came out to bash us and did just that, winning both games and the attention of WWE boss, Vince McMahon, in the process.

This was the same year that Samoa beat the Wallabies and that match was only a few weeks previous to our visit. So the Samoan lads were on a roll. It was also the same Wallabies game where Rod Davies was picked ahead of me and was marking Alesana Tuilagi.

I was a little pissed about the selection and wanted to prove myself to Robbie Deans, so I gave him a buzz after that Wallabies game and said we are playing Samoa and that I'd be marking big Tuilagi and to keep an eye out for me.

This was my opportunity to prove I was capable of playing rugby at the highest level and I gave it a red-hot go, bagging a bit of meat and scoring a good shot on Tuilagi. And that hit will go down in the history books – or Mum's scrapbook at least.

The big unit burst through the line like a fat bloke to the bathroom after a Chinese banquet and I've come across from fullback determined to push him out. But instead of him just running for the corner, he angled directly at me and went for the bump. But I couldn't just lay down. I'd just given it to Robbie and had the eyes of the world – or at least Mum – on me.

MY HEAD WAS LYING ON HIS CHEST, LIKE A COUPLE OF YOUNG GIRLS AT CAMP.

When I woke up a few seconds later we were both over the sideline and a little confused. My head was lying on his chest, like a couple of young girls at camp. I'd done it!

I got my balance and stood up and looked down at the giant lying before me and just shook my head, thinking, 'That's shithouse! You should have absolutely steam rolled me!'

A dude that size, he had a lot of advantages on me. But this badger's got heart. And perhaps a little luck on my side.

Anyhow, in summing up, I basically beat The Rock and should be a WWE Superstar.

"THE BOYS WERE ON IT LIKE SEAGULLS AT A TIP. "

TRANSLATION: 'Ever been to a dump and seen all those seagulls covering the mound? That's what the boys' defence reminded me of today – they covered the bloke like he was a mound of food and they were seagulls.'

POSTCARD SHOT

After copping a hammering by the Samoans, the boys got a well deserved day off. I mean, finally! The island holiday I'd dreamed of ever since watching *Castaway* – just the clear water, some lovely coconuts, a man and his balls. Perfect.

So on our day off we drove around the main island when I spotted a palm tree that has grown about seven metres out horizontally to the water. My immediate instincts screamed 'classic postcard pic'. And when I think of postcards there's only one Queensland classic that comes to mind – 'bum, titty, bum'.

So without hesitation I launched myself from

> **WHEN I THINK OF POSTCARDS THERE'S ONLY ONE QUEENSLAND CLASSIC THAT COMES TO MIND – 'BUM, TITTY, BUM'.**

the car, dropped me duds and climbed out over the water with the old twig 'n' berries swaying in the breeze like God intended. Of course, it was far from a good sight for the poor bastard taking the pic. Spare a thought for the confused locals, too.

Then all of a sudden I hear one of the said locals yelling at me from 100 metres away as she began power walking towards me with the ferocity of a mum determined to drag her kid back home for dinner after the street lights went on.

And lemme tell ya, it's tough to balance on a palm tree four metres above razor sharp coral at the best of times, let alone when trying to pull your bog catchers on in a hurry.

Like Ronda Rousey, she looked scary and she meant business. That Samoan strength isn't exclusive to the men, you know.

But with a turn of speed and a sneaky side step I managed to elude her and we quickly hit the frog and toad and headed back to base where the team manager was waiting for us in the carpark. We quickly discovered that news travels surprisingly fast for a place that claims to run on 'island time'.

The manager opens up the van door and quickly informs us that the hotel had heard reports of disturbances involving nudity emanating from a van very similar to ours. 'Who was it?' he exclaimed.

I waited for a bit then put the hand up. And he wasted no time escorting me directly to the coach's quarters.

'What the f*&k do you think you're doing?' were the first words that spat from his mouth. 'Do you realise what this could do to the Western Force name? Tell me what you were thinking?'

Never one to beat around the bush – unless we're talking foreplay – I quickly replied: 'I was going for a postcard shot. Honest, mister.'

The manager could barely hold a straight face and released a small burst of air to suggest he was on the verge of cracking. 'Nude?' the coach questions. I nodded. Just waiting to hear the 'D' word – disciplinary action – I cringed.

Then with a half serious scowl combined with a half smile he just says: 'Bloody hell, I don't want to hear about this any more.' So I quickly bailed, the snap safely in hand. I've still got the shot and it's a pearler.

"LAST YEAR WAS A BIT, UH, HOW YOU GOIN', BUT UM, NAH WE'RE GOOD NOW. "

TRANSLATION: 'No point looking back. All you'll get is a sore neck.'

TRANSLATION OF THE TRANSLATION: 'You can't change the past. Better off looking to the future.'

DAD AND THE BIG C

A lot of this book focuses on the good times and if you haven't noticed already, there's been plenty of them. But we all go through a tough one from time to time and for me, the hardest day of my life came back in September 2014.

It was a beautiful afternoon in Perth and I burned down to the beach for a classic Indian Ocean sunset after training. Life couldn't get any better. And then it got a helluva lot worse.

I got a call from the old boy and immediately knew something was off. His voice was flat and he wasn't talking with the same energy I'd grown well used to.

I flat-out asked him what the go was and that's when he responded with the words no friend, parent, colleague or even enemy wants to hear – 'I've got cancer.'

He'd been for a check-up a few weeks earlier after experiencing a few dull pains in the guts and the test came back bad – he had stage four terminal prostate cancer, and it had spread.

'How long?' I asked. 'A few years, the doc reckons,' he responded.

It hit me straight away and all the things consuming my life – selection, traffic, rent and all that, didn't seem to matter any more. My first thoughts were of my little brother and sister who depend on him. Then the thought of the father–son time that I wanted more of. Having eight kids on only his income didn't allow for as much quality one-on-one time as I wanted. Dad has always done his best, which I think is beyond most could imagine. I mean, eight kids! That's a bloody scrum!

DAD HAS ALWAYS DONE HIS BEST, WHICH I THINK IS BEYOND MOST COULD IMAGINE.

But my old man is the original Honey Badger. The original underdog. And he's beaten the odds all his life. I told him we'd fight and in his damned voice he says, 'Of course we will. We'll will give it a good crack.'

My biggest fear was his old-school mindset, because he isn't exactly known for his flexibility. And I thought that might affect the help he was willing to seek, but he would surprise me!

Personally, from what I've seen of chemotherapy, it really knocks the body about and can leave people suffering a range of different health issues for the rest of their lives. I'm often sceptical of expensive treatments. Call me a hippy, an idealist or a dreamer, but I'd really like Dad to be open to different approaches, beyond what the medical profession and pharmaceutical industry prescribes.

I will try to find a way to help Dad overcome the cancer and we're working on options now. The show ain't over, he'll have a crack. I know he will.

"YEAH MATE, IT'S BLOODY OUTSTANDING, YOU KNOW. THAT BLOODY SEA OF BLUE, JUST GETS RIGHT UP YA AND GIVES YA THE STRENGTH. "

TRANSLATION: 'A shout out to the Force fans. We love ya.'

MONGOLIAN ADVENTURE PART: 1

In 2014 while playing in Japan, I was lucky enough to be invited to play for the Barbarians against the Wallabies – keeping in mind I wasn't eligible at the time to play for Australia. Better yet, the week before I was set to leave for England my Japanese team had a bye. And that means only one thing in professional sport – holiday!

The sheila had dreams of covering Europe but there was only one destination on my travel agenda – Mongolia.

I'd heard great stories of golden eagles, one of nature's deadliest birds of prey, attacking and defeating snakes, deer and wolves. And how since the middle ages Mongolians have trained them to be hunters for their villages.

So I booked one day in advance then launched. I told the sheila my plans and that if she wanted in there would be no

'YOU'LL HAVE TO BOG IN THE DIRT' I TOLD HER AND SHE AGREED TO THE TERMS

complaining about there being no dunnies or showers. 'You'll have to bog in the dirt' I told her and she agreed to the terms – a good sport. All was set. Or so I thought…

As we boarded the steel chicken I get an email from the tour organiser saying 'DO NOT BOARD THIS FLIGHT – your visa won't be ready and you will be arrested on arrival'.

Nonplussed and having already ordered an assortment of food and beverages, I figured I could do a night or two in the slammer. I mean, I don't get much time off in my job so I was willing to take risks to get 'em.

Hell, I had the whole flight and a heap of tinnies to come up with a plan and as we landed I handed the missus all the money and told her to go and stay in the capital, Ulaanbaatar, until a flight could be booked to get her out of there.

We land. And with my heart racing I hear customs officers calling my name out. But this is Mongolia and they've got no idea what I look like, so I decide to run the gauntlet and bypass them and head straight to the information desk. With the charisma of James Bond, I begin a wonderful story of heartfelt innocence featuring minimal truth and come clean on the whole thing. And to my surprise, she bought it! Not only was I allowed to stay but she escorted me to my bags and I may or may not have left with her number…

I was in! I'd escaped a prison sentence. And now I had some hunting to do.

We caught a two-hour domestic flight to our next destination and then hit the frog and toad for three hours covering all kinds of vast landscape – flats, riverbeds and massive mountain ranges – before arriving at our humble destination in the middle of bumf**k nowhere. I couldn't have been more excited!

" YEAH LOOK, THERE'S A COUPLE OF BIG HOOAHS GETTING ABOUT. "

TRANSLATION: 'They have some monstrous players. I'm a little scared.'

MONGOLIAN ADVENTURE PART: 2

We were immediately greeted by the host family offering a bounty of produce – goat cheese, horse milk and vodka. The vodka was to help you forget about the horse milk.

It was middle ages luxury. We slept on the floor of a traditional nomadic tent and I was having one helluva night's sleep before being woken by the sound of a camel being milked.

Figuring it must be early morning, I decide to duck out to empty the tank. And at this time it's semi-dark so I just stuck my head out the metre-high door only to rub noses with a yak! It scared the living shit out of me. The bastard's horns were big enough to cause some serious damage and I didn't want to be no yak's bitch.

So I turned on the pace, got past the bastard and the camels and was just 15 metres away from the house when I heard a familiar yet

I DIDN'T WANT TO BE NO YAK'S BITCH.

sickening noise beside me. Fearing the worst, I turned around only to have my greatest fears realised – it was the 60-year-old lady of the house snapping one off right next to me! My nostrils took a real hit and I wasn't sure if I should greet her or pretend I didn't see her and just start walking. I chose the latter. But the image and sound of an old lady dropping a 2 x 4 and looking up at me with a bung eye will remain with me even after I'm dead. And I considered ending it there and then.

By now, I was well awake and jumped into a stream of melted snow to freshen up and scrub myself clean.

MONGOLIAN ADVENTURE PART: 3

Now cleansed of the surprise stench and having laid some groundwork of my own, it was time to hunt. By horseback we headed out into the mountains with our guides and golden eagle and falcon handlers. Watching those glorious birds circle and swoop for foxes and rabbits was nothing short of sensational.

In one of the hunts we were a couple hundred metres up on a ridge when a fox shot out from a cave underneath and just pinned his ears back. It was on! Our guide galloped to the edge of the ridge, removed the helmet from the eagle's head and within seconds the big bastard launched off the cliff just screaming and tearing down on the fox.

The fox zigged and zagged like Wendell Sailor but it was outmatched, outclassed. But full credit to the shifty fox, because as the eagle zeroes in he decided to give it one last effort and turned to face the eagle head-on and attacked.

HE DECIDED TO GIVE IT ONE LAST EFFORT AND TURNED TO FACE THE EAGLE HEAD-ON AND ATTACKED.

These eagles have claws the size of a man's hand and it gripped the face of the fox shut with one foot and the other gripped the guts. It was all but game over. But it's important not to let the birds suffer injury during the hunt, so the eagle handler must hurry down to catch and dispatch the fox quickly so the eagle won't be hurt in the struggle. It was glorious.

We celebrated that night with sing-alongs. I attempted to show my vocal prowess but I struggle with English let alone Mongolian chants. But with the bulk vodka I provided no one seemed to care and the old man and I were best mates.

It was one of my best tours yet and highly recommended. Go on, pull your finger out and book it!

Oh yeah, that week in Mongolia was my prep for the game against the Wallabies at Twickenham. Best training camp ever.

TACKLE PRACTICE

When I was around 12 years old, Dad would take me and other kids around to our cousin Ben's farm when it was time to muster the sheep. No wonder the Kiwis hate me…

He would be able to get most of them but there was always a handful that were as defiant of authority as we were. You know, harder to catch than a cab at 3 am.

So we would be sent in to bring 'em in. The kind of job as an adult you'd dread but the type of mission a kid lives for.

Dad and Ben would have a few tins and watch our attempts, Dad just praying for that *Funniest Home Video* moment. I was dick-high to a midget and a flat-out

I WAS DICK-HIGH TO A MIDGET AND A FLAT-OUT 50 KG WRINGING WET

50 kg wringing wet, up against fully grown sheep – not to mention a ram! It was the biggest bloody sheep I had seen, with horns to intimidate anyone. But it wasn't the ugliest thing I've wrestled over the years… Which is a perfect segue to the ewes – the female sheep.

They were quickest but didn't have an aggressive streak in 'em, so they were easier to get in. I would herd them to a corner and charge them, dive and try and grab their legs. But it wasn't that effective. And just to be clear, we're talking about a 12-year-old boy and sheep…

I was quick to work out that, if you dive and grip the wool first then while they are dragging you, pull them to the ground then sit them on an angle with their bum on the deck while holding the front two legs, this would make them become still and easier to manoeuvre. The job was almost done and I was looking like the protégé of the famous bloke from Snowy River.

But then there was the bloody ram. Like a big kid in the schoolyard, the plan was to tire him out before taking him down. And as I made my approach he pointed his horns toward me and paused. It was now or never and I continued to charge in, adamant I'd called his bluff. Wrong.

All of a sudden he charged me and the shoe was on the other foot. I took off like a schoolkid from class and in that split second the ram knew he had the mental edge on me. I could see it in his eyes.

But more fearful of the carry-on from everyone that would ensue if I gave up 'scared', I faced the beast yet again. And this time as it came at me I braced for impact and grabbed his horns at the same time.

IN THAT SPLIT SECOND THE RAM KNEW HE HAD THE MENTAL EDGE ON ME.

I was tossed, smashed, dragged around and grazed but I hung on for dear life and managed to flip him.

I don't know who was more buggered but my reputation was intact. Forget the Kiwis, if you need a sheep taken down, I'm your man. Wait, I'm not sure that comes across right?

"YOU'RE AS TOUGH AS WOODPECKER LIPS."

TRANSLATION: 'Woodpeckers are birds that use their own beaks to break through wood and make houses and find food. You get that? They use their own lips to break wood. You can't get tougher.'

THE CAFFEINATED CASHIER

I was 15 years old and fed up with labouring so caught myself a job at the air-conditioned shelter known as Woolworths – one of only two remaining employers in Australia nowadays…

Anyhow, like any kid, I worked weekend and night shifts after school and this one day I was particularly buggered. I'd had all but no sleep from a party the night before and was about to start an eight-hour shift.

And so it would be the day I had my first coffee. And make no mistake, it drew plenty of attention in the lunch room as I made it.

Not having made a coffee before, I nonchalantly filled three-quarters of a styrofoam cup with ground coffee, with just enough room for hot water. 'That's how they do it in the ads, right?'

I was pretty confident in my coffee making ability even as an amateur, so when the deli lady raised an eyebrow and asked if I needed some help, I gave her a quicksmart 'No thanks, I'm good, lady'.

'WHY DO PEOPLE DO THIS TO THEMSELVES?' I THOUGHT TO MYSELF.

I tried to mix it but it was very lumpy. But being late as usual I had no time for stirring, so I skolled the thing and felt every scratch on the way down. 'Why do people do this to themselves?' I thought to myself. And as far as I knew, it wasn't even working. I was just as tired as I was when I made the damn thing.

Then all of a sudden, about 20 minutes after consumption, the whites of my eyeballs suddenly bulged with a simultaneous bing! And from nowhere, I was on the burst!

I was fanging three items per second through the till, flinging cans of baked beans from one hand to the other like a cocktail barman and passing the scanner and beeping all the way through.

Customers were stoked and getting out of the joint in record time. And all was well until an hour had passed. And without any brekky, my world began crumbling like the Greek economy. I then hit the lowest low and picking up every item was a punishment.

I WAS FANGING THREE ITEMS PER SECOND THROUGH THE TILL

But two momentous things happened that day: History was made when stats showed I had achieved the fastest scan rate in store history. And I realised the only way to beat the coffee comedowns was to keep drinking the bastards until the coffee pot ran dry.

"I'M LOOKING FORWARD TO GETTING OUT THERE AND SEEING PLENTY MORE OF THE SEED IN 2014."

TRANSLATION: 'A seed is shaped like a football. A seed is also imperative to growing something – like a score. Therefore, seeds are vital to survival in life and sport.'

QUICK FIRE

I didn't mind working at Woolies as a checkout chick but I sure as shit didn't take it seriously. Which, suffice to say, the store managers didn't take too kindly.

With my rugged good looks and boyish charm, I could generally get by with a smile and was on good terms with the hierarchy. Until one day when it all came crashing down.

It was Christmas time and my supervisor, who at this stage I was on good terms with, approached with reindeer antlers for me to wear on my head. I wasn't having any of it, so after barely a glance I quickly turned away to serve a customer. 'Nick! You have to wear it. It's company policy and part of the uniform,' she says.

Never one to get into a barney, I say 'righto' and keep going about my business – working sans the reindeer antlers. You think that was the end of it?

'You had better have this on by the time I finish handing these out,' she says. And when she returns a few minutes later to see the antlers haven't moved, she just stares at me as I shrug my shoulders and say 'Can't do it'. I've since learned that women don't take kindly to that response. Nor bosses. Nor people in general, in fact. 'If I decide to go to head office you could be fired,' she continues. To which I reply: 'Do what ya gotta do, babe. I can't bring myself to do it.'

I'VE SINCE LEARNED THAT WOMEN DON'T TAKE KINDLY TO THAT RESPONSE.

Thinking that was the end of it, I went about my day triumphantly as all the other poor bastards were forced to stand eight hours straight wearing fake antlers. I mean, as if working the registers wasn't bad enough?

But as I successfully finished my shift without the assistance of the precious antlers, the manager approached angrily: 'Nick, why wouldn't you do it?' To which I replied: 'There comes a time in a man's life when he has to make a stand for what he believes in. And for me, this is that time.'

I was yet to celebrate my 16th birthday.

THE UNEXPECTED

I don't expect this to make sense to you right now, but the information I'm about to give you will make sense come the end of the story that follows. In some juvenile circles, and made famous by a movie or two, there's a game called 'Goat' – it's basically a penis-pranking game amongst male friends where you lure an unsuspecting mate into looking at your junk without expecting it and then ridicule them for being a pervert.

Continue…

So, Grand Plaza is a major shopping centre in Browns Plains, south of Brisbane. And occasionally when I'm home we slip down to do some shopping for essentials like beer, wine, steak and beer. And to just have a gander at who's who in the zoo. You never know who you might spot there – maybe a performance from whoever came ninth on Australian Idol in 2009. The joint is like that scene from the bar in *Star Wars* – creatures of all shapes and sizes, great and small. And plenty of Ed Hardy. It's out there!

Anyhow, after snagging a shake from Wendy's, a few cinnamon doughnuts fresh off the conveyor belt, we took off home for an afternoon of carb loading.

We were driving behind a beat-up old yellow van and the standard jokes came to mind: 'If the van's a rockin', don't come a knockin'; 'Never trust a van with no windows'; and 'If you see something, say something.'

And sure enough, no sooner had the van pulled up at the lights than the rear door burst open and out the back launched a tied body! Holy shit! On second look, we thought it was a dog and then on third look realised it was in fact a goat. Phew. But the poor bastard was tied around the neck and only his back legs touched the road.

NOW, ME AND THE OLD MAN LIKE HUNTING, BUT WE'RE NOT ONES FOR ANIMAL CRUELTY.

Now, me and the old man like hunting, but we're not ones for animal cruelty.

So, just as the light turned green, the old man threw the car into park, jumped out, sprinted and started belting on the van's driver-side window.

The bloke driving was understandably shit-scared. He'd be forgiven for thinking Dad was a homeless man attempting to wash his windscreen with nothing more than a mouthful of spit and his singlet. And in a deep Middle Eastern accent he says: 'What you want?'

Well, Dad, cool as a cucumber, just says: 'Mate, I think your goat fell out!'

Time stood still as I realised what I had just witnessed. Lucky for Dad, the driver didn't call him out for being a pervert.

The goat was saved. And it still brings a smile to my dial when I think of Dad telling a bloke his twig and berries had fallen out.

"YEAH, MATE. I BLOODY WAS LIKE A RAT UP A DRAINPIPE IN ONE OF THEM RUNS THERE."

TRANSLATION: 'Rats can run up drainpipes. But only if they gather enough speed. That's how fast I was running out there. Quick enough to run vertical.'

BILLABONG HOPPING

If there's the chance of fish or the risk of danger, I'm more than eager to get involved. So when my brother suggested heli-fishing, I jumped at the chance to throw a line in from height – like that Dreamworks cartoon before movies when that kid drops a line into the ocean from the half moon he's sitting in…

Basically, it involves whacking all of your gear, beer, bait and ammo into a chopper and heading to the billabongs and small bodies of water south of Darwin.

And given I'd just broken my bloody hand in a match against Argentina, ruling me out of the next leg of the 2013 Rugby Championship, I was only too happy to go fishing and forget about it all.

It was me, Dad, my brother Luke, a mate of ours named

Braedon, two choppers and a pilot who went by the self-proclaimed name of 'Batman'. And with the choppers fuelled up, doors removed and blades pumping, it was time to get the hell out of Darwin and find us some fish. Nothing was safe. We had everything short of infrared.

Ripping across the lowlands of the Northern Territory, wind in your hair and stubby in hand, I felt like Fabio – the most beautiful man in the cosmos. And quite honestly, taking into consideration the crew I was travelling with, it wasn't far from the truth. Dad's got a

I FELT LIKE FABIO – THE MOST BEAUTIFUL MAN IN THE COSMOS.

face like a robber's dog and Luke's has been described as a half-sucked mango. Anyhow, now to drag something in!

Batman buzzed the billabongs to make the crocs jump. But I reckon we jumped higher. Those giant amphibious rigs were just as hungry for a feed as we were, so we got outta there quick smart.

And soon enough, buzzing along at tree-top level, we spotted our pond of domination. So down we went.

It reminded me of one of the old man's Vietnam stories about three against 30,000. But in this story it was we, the invaders, who were outnumbered. But we weren't out-gunned.

We had more rods out than the Lang Park urinals at halftime. And with our lures to the ready, we cast our lines. And whack! First flick I've hooked me a big ol' grunter. Dad then proceeded to pull my lure from his leg and I cast again… This time, I hooked me a real grunter – one that didn't swear at me.

And just as I got him to the bank, to claim the first trophy of the day, a bloody big lizard grabbed hold of it. Suffice to say, I shit myself almost immediately and let him have that one.

The old boy was first to drag one in – a nice barra. And he wasted no time hooting and hollering. He was making more noise than two skeletons doing the Macarena on a tin roof. I reminded him that mine was bigger. 'And where is it, mate?' he said in the cold tone of a British soccer hooligan.

I dropped my head and before Dad had a chance to rub it in any further, we set off for the coast. Soaring along the coastline the ocean was teeming with rays, crocs and Noah's arks. So we headed back inland and this time, it was my time to shine.

We settled on an inlet about 20 kilometres west of Darwin. I made a textbook cast with just the right choice of small plastic and whack! It was on, 20 kilos of leaping excellence on the other end of the line and the bastard was all mine. I swear Dad shed a solitary tear.

'How you like them apples?' I thought as I grinned at my loser companions. 'Who's Batman now, pussies?'

I could already see dinner, the beers, the story, but I didn't see the croc. One hit and it took the backend of my barra clean off. Another hit and it removed all evidence.

Its work was done. So was mine. But Dad was only just getting started with rubbing it in.

" **I'D BE 37 OR SOMETHING FOR THE NEXT ONE AND I'D NEED FOUR FACELIFTS AND A BUM TUCK TO BE A SHOT.** "

TRANSLATION: 'Don't be stupid.'

ALL BLACKS BLACK EYE

Rugby players don't often start fights. But if forced to, they'll finish them.

Once you start to get recognised, be it local or nationally, a lot of juiced-up blokes like to test themselves against you.

My first experience was in 2006. I'd been in Sydney for a few months and we'd just had a good win at Coogee Oval. Better yet, the Bledisloe Cup was on and I, my roommate Luke Bertram and buddy Blair Frendin headed to the clubhouse to watch the game over a few cold ones.

To my delight, the Wallabies won. And with two victories in one day, we headed to a local burger joint for a quick Bruce Reid before getting on the launch pad and pressing the button for a big night out.

All was well. We were reminiscing the finer points of both games and bangin' a burger in when a bloke in an All Blacks jersey and one too many under the belt wanders over to our table and takes a chip right from Blair's plate. Now, from what the internet has shown me, I understand Kiwi folk love their 'fush and chups'. But taking food from another man's plate – let alone a stranger's – is just not on.

We ignored it. But the bloke thought he'd help himself to another. And on this attempt, his hand was met with Blair's, who pushed the bloke's hand away and kindly asked him to beat it.

Well, old mate had no intentions of leaving quietly and started swearing and causing a scene in the joint. I hadn't copped this much heat in a restaurant since I refused to pay $16 for a beer at that small sushi joint in Surry Hills – Nobu I think it is?

So he threatens to bash Blair, which in essence is Blair's fault. I told him you always sit with your back to the wall… Anyhow, Blair stands up and tells the bloke to beat it once more. But this time, the Kiwi swung a packed lunch and Blair – school judo champion from the year before – ducked and landed a beauty right on old mate's scone. The silly bloke was hammered, and went crashing through table and chairs, landing on the deck with a busted beak and a split eye.

I WASN'T ABOUT TO MISS OUT ON A NIGHT OUT OVER SOME SOGGY CHIPS

He gingerly gets up, claret everywhere and as Blair was moving towards him I jumped between them. I'd seen enough. I held them apart and said to Blair: 'He's done, mate. He's had enough.' And no sooner had I turned to the Kiwi bloke to say it's over when he king hit me in the temple! And it bloody hurt.

Now, I love my grub as much as, if not more, than the next bloke. But I wasn't about to miss out on a night out over some soggy chips.

So I grabbed Blair and Luke and made a beeline for the pub – 'cause I knew the swelling was only gonna get bigger and I wouldn't be let in in half an hour's time.

The security guard asked what happened to my eye and I replied: 'Got a few bumps during our win today for Randwick.' It worked a treat.

I was always taught to steer clear of fights. Dad always said that no one really wins in a fight, but if someone starts one, you finish it.

The black eye turned out to be a biggie and, given I barely got tackled – as per usual – that day, I'm not sure if my boss and coach bought the story. But I would take a hit for my mate any day. Good mates are rare these days.

> **"I'M GONNA HAVE A TRUCKLOAD OF PUDDING AND UH, OLD MUM'S GOOD ON THE COOK TOO SO, DAD'S GOT THE TUCKER READY OVER THERE AND MUM AND DAD ARE GONNA WORK TOGETHER AND FORM A MASSIVE FEED AND ER, I'M GONNA COME IN AND DOMINATE IT."**

TRANSLATION: 'I'm real hungry after that and the oldies have promised me a feed. They better not disappoint.'

SPIDER'S WEB

It was 2010 and I was playing for Randwick, where the rugby club had put me up in Coogee with my mate Blair Frendin. And for once, this wasn't a place where police tape and sidewalk chalk were a daily given.

Me and Blair were living the golden life only 250 metres from the beach on the main street. We spent our time-off surfing, chasing birds, exploring and going to Daryl Braithwaite concerts and chasing older birds. It truly was a great time to be alive.

There was a tucker joint that went by the name of 'Five O's' and we frequented the dive for dinner 'cause it had a good-sized feed dirt cheap. Me and Blair didn't have very high standards in any of our pursuits – culinary or otherwise… But the owner's staff hiring policy certainly wasn't anything to sneeze at.

Once we were confident that the two waitresses who worked there considered us 'regulars', we worked up the courage to put on our James Bond suits (Fun fact: James Bond gets all his quality suits from Lowes) and engage in charismatic repartee in the hope of luring them in. Nothing sinister, we just wanted to begin the courting process.

JAMES BOND GETS ALL HIS QUALITY SUITS FROM LOWES

The two birds were ginger ninjas and cool as cucumbers, so one night we invited them to our joint for pre-drinks before a game – jokes! – before heading out.

Hours later Blair and I find ourselves playing *Call of Duty* on Xbox – a female aphrodisiac in any language – having totally forgotten about our invitation.

Then a shriek! We were suddenly horrified by the sound of blood-curdling screams coming from the dark and dingy 20-metre stretch of putrid path that one had to take to get to our front door. It was right then we remembered the girls and also that the booby traps we would set daily for our unwitting teammates to come a mischief were still active!

We rushed outside and it looked like something from *Lord of the Rings*. The girls were tangled up in the fishing lines we had set at various heights, that were connected to a suspended pushbike and bucket full of vacuum dust.

The poor girls had fallen – the traps worked perfectly, just quietly – but were oddly still somewhat suspended by the array of lines. All we could do was laugh at the sheer confusion and disbelief on their faces.

After they brushed off the vacuum dust, we proceeded inside and as you can imagine they weren't short of questions. Or too stoked that we wanted to finish *Call of Duty*.

And to my surprise, all these years later, one of those red-headed beauties is still putting up with Blair after getting tangled in our web.

But as her friend found out, no bird can tame this brumby. (*Disclaimer: By brumby, I mean wild horse. And that suggestion does in no way pertain to my relationship – perceived or otherwise – to the ACT Brumbies, which may or may not be a rugby franchise.*)

"JUST LIKE THAT KID THAT FELL OUTTA THE TREE YA KNOW, HE JUST WASN'T IN IT."

TRANSLATION: 'He didn't stand a chance.'

THONG
THEFT

Long before it was trendy to have driftwood signs hanging in your home promoting 'Live, laugh, love' and whatever other affirmations the insecure and obviously miserable house-owner deems worthy, the old man flew one flag. A motto, if you will. It read: 'A man's thongs are his greatest possession'.

At least, that's what he told us. We never saw the thing. But he put the fear of Dad into us and from an early age we learned to worship, above all else, our double pluggers.

Like a good guard dog, Dad would say, thongs sit at the doorway, ever ready for action. Because with a simple flip of the toe, the over-turned plugger is ready to be stood on, put into action and provide the barrier between foot and bindi. Between gay abandon and painful pebbles. Between your big toes and bitumen.

Between a night out at the RSL and sitting on the footpath with a tallie (that's a long neck to you southerners). You get the picture…

So with that in mind, as a family, we took thong theft more seriously than a small town takes UFO sightings. In short, thong theft is a dog act.

But for some reason, every bugger who has ever fronted up to my house has seemingly done so barefoot before feeling the need to flee with my prized possessions. My most valuable assets. My thongs.

In some ways, I'm thankful to them. How else do you think I learned to run so quickly? By chasing the bastards down is how.

Anyhow, a few years back I'd had enough. I'd witnessed something like five casualties in the space of a month and decided to do something drastic – go to Target.

As luck would have it, good old Tar-shay had a special on single pluggers – $1 a pair. They were genuine 1972 prices that I couldn't pass up.

So I laid out two lobsters and got meself 40 pairs. It was time for a social experiment involving thongs, random house guests and grubby blokes. But this was no porno.

And sure enough, they took the bait. Every time a pair went missing, I'd keep quiet and deposit another by the stairs. The old man laid down the odds – reckoned we'd be out in six months. I scoffed at it and took that action, confident at least a few pairs of the classic blue/white combo would see another Christmas.

But like errant cattle stumbling onto the wrong property, I was shocked. Four months! Four months is all it took for my so-called friends and family to bleed me dry of God's greatest creation. Now, put that into consideration. That's 10 pairs a month at 2.5 pairs a week.

And not only was I out of 40 pairs of pluggers but I owed a pineapple to the old man, too. It was a $90 loss and the day I lost my innocence forever.

Yep, forget finding out the Easter Bunny, Santa Claus and cartoons weren't real. That was the day I discovered just how low humans will stoop.

I remember looking at the last pair with a head like a beaten favourite, knowing the dream was over. And life would never be the same again. They, too, were gone at the very next BBQ.

"THAT LOOK ON YOUR FACE LIKE SOMEONE ASKED ME TO CLEAN THE TOILET AND I WAS JUST BLOODY GOIN' FOR GOLD."

TRANSLATION: 'Are you f*&king serious, right now?'

BARBARIANS VS AUSTRALIA 2014

I'd been playing in Japan for a few months confusing the hell out of the locals and thought I had left Australian Rugby behind.

Then came the call: 'Badge, do you want to play for the Barbarians in London?'

Shit yeah. Who wouldn't? Playing for Bah-Bahs is akin to 1980s rugby in that training largely consists of a few beers – for bonding's sake, of course – and a decent pay packet. I immediately agreed to the deal and *then* found out we were playing against Australia. Still, too good of an offer to refuse. I'd have played against Twickenham's Under-15 side if it meant re-uniting with a few of the boys from back home and having a beer with some of the international heroes.

I arrived on the Wednesday before the big game and I was absolutely cooked. I'd just finished that 10 days in Mongolia hunting foxes on horseback – with an eagle. I'd spent every night sleeping on a dirt floor and hadn't seen a porcelain dunny or otherwise in what seemed like years. It was a nice change not to have to dig a hole before dropping off the kids.

Anyway, no rest for the wicked. Sir John Kirwan, our coach, was a good bloke. He made sure we had a fat time and training was kept to a minimum – just how we liked it.

The game drew almost 55,000 and they were pumped. I was a little confused as what to do when they played the Aussie anthem over the speakers but without shame I belted it out anyway.

The game was flat-out. We called this random move we'd remembered from our 15-minute training session and I scored under the posts. There were three of us going for the ball but it was yours truly who grabbed the cheese and planted it. Very arsey!

It was a strange feeling playing against Australia. I had always been proud to wear the gold jersey and now the shoe was on the other foot. Actually, that analogy doesn't make sense. The jersey was literally on the other team and here I was tackling my countrymen. Or at least making sure the forwards did it for me.

And I tell ya what, it was a helluva nice experience to have the Euro crowd cheering me on instead of giving it to me. The crowd loved the game and really backed us in.

My old man, brother Nathan, manager Josh, cousin Dane and a host of mad Norwegian buggers swelled the crowd. There was much yahooing when we caught up to 40–36. Keep in mind, the blokes we were playing had been training twice daily, sans the beers.

Unfortunately, we were beaten by them – for reasons I just mentioned above – but it was a great game and a lot of fun.

After the game we roared into the official function. I'd organised six tickets for my crowd but we managed to smuggle in 18. My sleight of hand knows no limits.

Security tried to stop a few but Dad quickly stepped in: 'It's OK, they're with me!'

The old shagger had an official-looking shirt printed that included the IRB logo and in small print underneath read: 'No association whatsoever'. But hey, if security guards could read they wouldn't be security guards. Jokes…

Anyhow, this shirt got him into most venues.

The next Bah-Bahs game was at Leicester and I was a bit sore, only lasting until halftime.

BUT HEY, IF SECURITY GUARDS COULD READ THEY WOULDN'T BE SECURITY GUARDS.

But what I accomplished in half a game takes most others 80 minutes anyhow, so I didn't feel too bad. Haha.

On the bus to our hotel after, all the new blokes had to sing or dance. And Sir John was brutal in his condemnation of the performers. He was like Simon Cowell but with the ability to punch the shit out of you, so you took his feedback on the chin or it'd be a fist there instead. No punches were thrown.

Back at the hotel and we had the usual court session. Nathan, Dad and I went up against John Kirwan and a couple of others in a boat race. And we bloody smashed 'em – and again for good measure. Then we belted out the song 'I'll Never Find Another Ewe' and that wound the Kiwis right up!

Suffice to say, Sir John didn't take too kindly to the fun-poking or the vocal rendition. Legend of a bloke, Sir John.

ORPHANAGE

If you've made it this far in the book, you'll find it's pretty obvious I enjoy a laugh as much, if not more, than the next bloke. But the Badge has a serious side, too. And the plight of other human beings is something I care deeply about.

I'd always had a sense of empathy but like many of us, struggled to find the ideal outlet for it. That was until a solo trip to Cambodia in 2011

TO SAY THESE KIDS HAVE BEEN DEALT A HARD HAND IS AN UNDERSTATEMENT.

changed everything, when during my journey I came across an orphanage that had flooded.

The ACODO orphanage in Siem Reap provides children whose parents have died with food, water and basic education. To say these kids have been dealt a hard hand is an understatement. I'm an adult and can't imagine not having my old man around, but somehow these young kids still had smiles on their faces. The kids would put on performances to raise money for the orphanage on a flat area just above the flood waters. It was a joy to watch. They were good little actors bouncing round with dragon suits on and others banging sticks in tune. But it was equally heart-wrenching hearing the stories of how they came to be there.

I spotted one kid who was quite reserved but knew what was going on. He had a strong presence and I was drawn towards him, hoping that boosting him would help boost the group. It was a matter of just seconds before I decided to sponsor Churit to a better life. And being in that orphanage was such a humbling experience that since then it has led me down roads trying to make this world a better place.

Everyone deserves a fair go. And I'm living proof that no matter where you come from, you can make a difference to someone's life. There's no excuse not to help make others' lives that little bit easier.

BUDGIE
SMUGGLERS

Ask any of my girlfriends and they'll tell you flat-out that despite my shortcummins (see what I did there?) I've always been good with my hands – in the kitchen, around the house and other areas…

Anyhow, that can all be attributed to my grommet rooster days growing up with my brothers and our passion for heading out bush and building tree houses – each bigger, better and higher than the last. Our talents knew no bounds.

We'd sneak some tools out of the old boy's shed and head out for a hard day's work knowing full well that others had

THE MORE EXTRAVAGANT THE TREE HOUSES GOT, THE MORE DANGEROUS THE BOOBY TRAPS BECAME.

their eye on our masterbuilt tree houses. As such, booby traps were a must. And the more extravagant the tree houses got, the more dangerous the booby traps became.

Deadliest of all were the booby traps we'd installed on our masterpiece – a four-storey tree house courtesy of my brother Nath. She was a beauty. A bush skyscraper.

It was a climb to get supplies up there and we'd go fully loaded with gear so we wouldn't have to repeat the journey, but once upstairs at penthouse level, we felt invincible. Invincible, I tell ya! So long as the winds weren't blowing.

WE WERE KINGS. GOLDEN GODS. LORDS OF OUR OWN DOMAIN.

We spent hours up there, just taking it all in. We were kings. Golden gods. Lords of our own domain. Well, you get the drift. Like our talents for building said abodes, our confidence, too, knew no bounds. Which is never a good thing for a bunch of adolescent grubs.

So one day Nath was on look-out and spots what can only be described as an intruder – possibly a sexual one on account of the man in question wearing nothing but worn-out joggers and a pair of budgie smugglers in an even sadder state than his Sauconys. It was a sight to behold and but a second went by before one of my brothers sang out from the top of his lungs: 'Put some pants on, ya weirdo!'

It seemed justified given the nearest beach was some 100 nautical miles away and he was running in the suburbs. But as you can expect, he didn't take too kindly to the insult.

So old mate spun on a dime and yelled back: 'Right, get down here! I'm gonna give you a hiding!'

Forget that. We took enough beatings from each other let alone having some stranger give us what for in our own tree house. So it was a no-brainer – we'd stay up high in the fortress and continue to taunt him.

WE'D STAY UP HIGH IN THE FORTRESS AND CONTINUE TO TAUNT HIM.

'Get stuffed!' one of the brothers screamed. To Tony Abbott's reply: 'Take me to your parents now!'

Was he bluffing? We didn't know. He was on a rager – the mental kind, sickos.

Bugger it! We decided to wait this one out. There was no sign of wind, we had a pocket full of Redskins and we could wait it out longer than he could. Until…

The weirdo threw caution to the wind and with his twig and berries dangling in the air began to climb the tree! 'Things just got real', I thought to myself. Because all of a sudden I was fearing for his safety and not ours.

Little did he know we were ready for such an intruder. And every fourth step on the timber ladder up was a fake – as in it wasn't nailed in.

'Haha, got the bastard', my brother yelled as the intruder took a tumble on the fourth. I hadn't seen a grown man in dick togs hit the

ALL OF A SUDDEN I WAS FEARING FOR HIS SAFETY AND NOT OURS.

ground that hard since Trevor Hendy was dumped by a wave in old Uncle Toby's Ironman.

He then threatened to cut down the tree – the next logical step by a man who thought it was okay to subject a family neighbourhood to the sight of his sweaty junk bounce up and down like a pogo stick.

However, at this stage I was shit scared and had a turtle head poking out and headbutting me undies. 'Would he actually do it?'

As he stormed off to retrieve his cutting utensil, I didn't want to be around to witness a bloke in that get-up wielding an axe or chainsaw. Surely it's an OH&S issue. And quite frankly, we couldn't take the chance that he might be serious so we bailed out and clapped it on all the way home in case he followed through with his plot.

He never caught us. And I suspect he thought twice before pulling on his budgie smugglers for his next jog.

FRUIT BATS

Argentina 2015. Wallabies tour.

After initially missing out on the Wallabies squad, it didn't take long for the coaching staff to come to their senses and realise they needed a colourful shepherd for their sheep – yours truly.

The bulk of the team went direct to Argentina in preparation for the game but I was entrusted with something far more important – reinforcing international relations – and stereotypes – between Australia and the good people of Chicago, USA.

Nic White joined me as assistant ambassador to the Windy City, where we did what Obama never could and united the entire population and convinced them to attend our match against the American Eagles – not Roger Ramjet's ones – later in the year.

And the locals took pretty kindly to yours truly, anointing me with what I understand was a traditional nickname – the Honey Bear. Nic had a real laugh until they gave him his nickname – Eeyore. Take that, you grumpy prick. Ha!

Anyhow, with our diplomacy mission a success, we joined the rest of the squad in Argentina where Nathan Grey and Stephen Larkham put the boys through some intense contact sessions.

I COULDN'T REMEMBER BEING THIS PHYSICAL WITH A HUMAN BEING SINCE THE SCHOOL DANCE.

I couldn't remember being this physical with a human being since the school dance.

Anyhow, the team was selected on a Wednesday morning and I wasn't included. It happens. But as an old unspoken tradition, those double ds (not playing) are generally inclined to head out for a couple of Britney Spears to bond and relax the mind a bit from the frustration of selection. And with a day off training on the Thursday, why not? I asked myself?

Six of us didn't get a start and Drew Mitchell – who did get a number – quickly named the us the 'fruit bats' and set the standard early for what would become an ongoing joke. Despite the label, we didn't go batshit crazy but we enjoyed the night thoroughly. We definitely made use of our nocturnal allowance.

The next morning, however, everyone was expected to attend recovery – which was a sauna and stretching session – then a team meeting. There were a couple of red eyes from the fruit bats. And at least one of us looked like he'd been hanging upside down from a ceiling all night. And for once, it wasn't me.

During the team meeting we did an exercise of closing your eyes and visualising winning the Rugby World Cup. I'm certain this is the same method John Eales and Michael Lynagh employed during their campaigns…

Anyhow, when the lights came back on there were still some fruit bats 'visualising' with eyes closed and breathing heavier than Darth Vader. The bats were cooked and just as the jersey presentation was taking place at the end Scott Higginbotham leant over and rested his head on me. And there was a spare seat between us, so that gives you an idea of the real-life size of the big unit. And his melon was right on my shoulder, like two schoolgirls on the bus home from camp. At first I thought he was joking, so I ignored it and just snuggled in, as I had my own internal battles. Then it went past a joke as I realised he wasn't just resting the lids but had deadset fallen asleep.

That's when my paternal instincts kicked in. I shifted to the spare seat between us to sit him up and tried to wake him up without a scene but the 'ding bat' had spent way too long in the sauna and didn't rehydrate, leaving him with with the pruned hands of an Oxford Street fortune teller. And a brow just as rough.

He came to a little while later having been curled up in the foetal position and we got some fluids into the poor bastard.

The meeting finished and Drew Mitchell leans in with that cheeky grin: 'That's standard fruit bats'.

" LAST YEAR WE WERE ALL SIZZLE AND NO STEAK, BUT NOW WE'RE OFF LIKE A BRIDE'S NIGHTIE. "

TRANSLATION: 'We were all talk and no action. Nothing is quicker than a bride's nightie coming off wedding night. That's how quick we've been off the mark this year.'

THE IDEAL DATE

Like any wild animal, the honey badger is on the constant lookout for a mate – of the sexual variety, that is. And unlike penguins, most are anything but monogamous. I must be the exception to the rule. Because one thing's for sure, this honey badger's mating ritual is a thing of legend.

See, it was a few years back when I legged it into the local Woolies on a Sunday arvo in search of the perfect roasted chicken for dinner – you know the ones, the chooks that have been in the heating bay since 6 am and are drier than The Caxton after Origin. But little did I know that I'd find the perfect chick – of the human variety, that is.

There she was, in the produce section – a glow of energy beaming out to the beat of her own drum. This Viking beauty – or

Scandinavian for the PC crowd – had all the credentials necessary for the job – beautiful big... eyes, plump and ripe... cheeks, a perfect perky... smile and a good rig to boot. The world stopped. Warrant's 'Cherry Pie' blasted from the imaginary speakers. My mind instantly became alive with transient beams of thought cascading toward her like a cosmic river of creation. I knew I had to propose a first date. The only question was how?

Honey Badger Mating 101 suggests a scrap with another male or two before physically dominating the much smaller female. But like I said, I'm the exception to the rule so I waited for the perfect opportunity. I surveyed this mystic beauty as she gracefully patrolled the produce section, selecting only the healthiest and most vibrant fruit and veg. And instead of launching like a fat kid on a cupcake, I walked with purpose and precision, emanating a calm, confident, nonplussed approach to the task. And right before I introduced myself, God herself reached down and parted the peaches and pears, my dreamboat knocking over the oranges and sending them cascading to the floor. She did her best to stop them from hitting the ground but in the process lost her footing! As she went arse over head, I dived in to catch her like a footy from going into touch and put in a brilliant turn of phrase: 'You've fallen for me already'.

GOD HERSELF REACHED DOWN AND PARTED THE PEACHES AND PEARS

Well, suffice to say, she appreciated the chat and put on the kind of smile to you'd see in a romantic comedy. And she loved it. So I told her I'd take her out for a Bruce Reid and she replied 'When?'. It was the first time I'd heard her speak and after hearing that Scando accent it was like a deaf kid hearing music for the first time – I was ecstatic. 'You ripper!'. On a roll, I said 'Why not right now?' And sure enough, we both saddled up in the Bulldog (blue Holden Rodeo single cab tray back and my first car) and I drive her to a 'secret' secluded beach.

I then proceeded to grab my 'special' basket, rip off the thongs and escort her down to the beach, the sand gently bonding the gaps between our toes as our spiritual connection did the same. I had her just where I wanted her – on the rug as I started a fire from friction (see Aboriginal tech) and then pulled out a bottle of the best red the bottom shelf of the local liquor store had to offer. For five minutes I waxed lyrical about the prestige of the said Queen Adelaide Cab Sav and explained to her how you can't buy it anymore – it was roughly the same amount of time it took for me to remove the $3.99 price sticker from the back of it.

I filled her glass with the 2014 classic, fresh off the press, then headed to the water with my spear in hand. As fate would have it, I speared a fish in record time and before she could Viber her oldies to let 'em know she'd found paradise with the Badge, I had the fish cleaned and gutted and roasting on the fire. And if you think she was impressed then, you should see her face when she tasted the big bastard – she nearly slid off the rug!

Suffice to say, she made it clear it was the best date she'd ever been on. And long story short, not wanting to spoil the night and out of respect for her, we shook the sand out of our hair like nothing else. Hey, I didn't want her to think I was a tease… Nah, jokes.

I was nothing short of a country gentleman and dropped her home to keep the experience beautiful and restore her faith in the male population.

Like any good fisherman, I released her back into the wild to live another day… Or did I? That's private, ya bastards!

CHRISTMAS IN JAPAN

It was Christmas 2014 in Fukuoka, Japan – that's pronounced 'fark-u-ok-ey'. And while the locals won't hesitate to shut down the main street to celebrate New Year's, they don't care too much for Christmas. Guess their dads never got 'em the remote control cars they wanted …

Anyhow, they were kind enough at my club, Coca-Cola, to let us have a little feed at the clubhouse and they even pretended to enjoy themselves. They're so damn polite, it's a beautiful thing to watch. And as the players and their families were gorging on the grub – your typical Christmas feast of sashimi and seaweed soup – I decided to sneak outside and climb into my Santa suit. It's one of three things I pack every trip.

YOUR TYPICAL CHRISTMAS FEAST OF SASHIMI AND SEAWEED SOUP

So clad in best red and white get-up, I walk outside the clubhouse and in an instant the kids see me and come tearing outside. For a second, I forgot I was wearing the suit and freaked. It's never a good look as an adult male to lure a bunch of kids to your side with a bag of lollies. So I turned and sprinted away, throwing the candy over my shoulder. Needless to say, the getaway sticks didn't let me down.

After successfully sneaking back inside the clubhouse without the kids apprehending me, I loaded the gifts I had wrapped on the table, making sure no one could see. I wanted it to be a surprise. Because one gift in particular was a ripper.

I'd wrapped a framed picture of Tim Bateman (ex-Hurricanes player) dressed as a woman that I snapped at a dress-up earlier in the year. And I addressed the gift to former All Black Solomon King's wife. I could barely contain myself as I asked Tim to hand out the presents for me on account of me being 'busy'. Nick, you genius!

I watched in muffled silence and in awe of myself as Tim handed the wrapped picture to Solomon's wife completely unaware that the card clearly stated the gift was from him.

She happily opened it up and like a woman who'd just found out her partner was cheating, her jaw dropped. She was shocked to see a framed picture of Tim in a skirt – and a card to match. Tim was equally confused and embarrassed.

They awkwardly stumbled through the type of conversation no married woman wants to have – unless she's on Ashley Madison

– as I laughed hysterically in the corner. Suffice to say, Solomon didn't take too kindly either. But my fun wasn't over yet.

Another present was addressed to a Japanese player we called 'Tui' – short for God knows what. The present was 'from' one of the coaches and when Tui unwrapped it to find 5 kilograms of cat biscuits he was bitterly confused and quickly approached the coach who denied any knowledge of it. Everyone was dumbfounded and then Tui looks around to see me pissing myself and approaches confused as ever: 'Badger san, me have no pet'. And I reply: 'You will next Christmas!'

That day's laughter added years to my life. And regardless of my trickery, the Red Sparks have been good to me and the Cola boys are good men.

"I'VE BEEN DOING IT [PLAYING SUPER RUGBY] A GOOD FIVE YEARS NOW. LUCKY FOR ME EVERY BUGGER FELL OVER AND I GOT A GIG."

TRANSLATION: 'I'm not comfortable talking about myself in a professional sense. I'd prefer to deflect that question with some self-deprecating humour. I'm just happy to be here.'

A FINAL WORD

Thanks for taking the time to have a gander at a few stories that tell a little of my life. I've been blessed with a great family and friends and a job that I enjoy.

Sure there are tough times for everyone and for anyone who plays sport at the top level there are hundreds who don't make it because of injury, bad luck, or because the right people weren't paying attention.

There are plenty of others who battle chronic illness and just to keep going is a real mission. These are people I admire, because of what they do and how they remind us of what's important.

Life is a great gift. Get out and get amongst it. Smile and find humour in your day because it's infectious and we're only here for a short time. Make the most of it and leave this place a little better than you found it.

A few years ago Dad was having dinner with my sister Bernadette in Cambodia. She'd just led Thailand in a test against Vietnam in netball and it was a good chance for them to catch up. He gave her some advice as they looked out over the Mekong River. Forgive yourself and forgive others.

Makes sense!

See ya round the ridges.

The Badger

THE HONEY BADGER

Get amongst my app on Apple and Google Play.

It's free and it will be the best money you've never spent!